FIRST LADIES

pil

Publications International, Ltd.

Images from Flickr.com, including photographs from the GPA Photo Archive, State Archives and Library of Florida, the Woodrow Wilson Presidential Library, and U.S. State Department; Library of Congress, Prints and Photographs Division, including photographs in the Harris & Ewing collection, the Carol M. Highsmith Archive, and the U.S. News & World Report magazine photograph collection; National Archives; National Park Service; Shutterstock.com; official White House photographs including photographs by Amanda Lucidon and Chuck Kennedy (page 300); Wikimedia Commons, including photographs by users Daderot and Pi3.124

Contributing Writers Sheryl DeVore and Jennifer Zeiger

ISBN: 978-1-64558-740-8

Manufactured in China.

8 7 6 5 4 3 2 1

Let's get social!

 @Publications_International

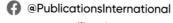 @PublicationsInternational

www.pilbooks.com

How much do you know about America's first ladies?
Since the presidency began, every president has had a
wife, daughter, or friend by his side who has variously
acted as adviser, host, or companion. All of them have
played a role in history, whether they were working
behind the scenes or standing at the podium.

Each first lady is profiled in the pages of this book, be-
ginning with Martha Washington and going all the way
to Dr. Jill Biden. You will learn about their childhoods
and married lives, their successes and failures, and the
marks they left on the presidency, the White House,
and the nation.

We are all familiar with the presidents' names. Now it
is time to learn more about the women at their sides!

Table of Contents

Martha Dandridge Custis Washington

Martha Dandridge was born to John Dandridge and Frances Jones on June 2, 1731. She was the eldest of eight children, and she grew up in comfort on the large Chestnut Grove plantation, not far from Williamsburg, Virginia.

Not long before her nineteenth birthday, Martha married 38-year-old Daniel Parke Custis, one of the wealthiest people in the area. Custis died just seven years later, in 1757. It was about one year later that Martha Custis, now a widow, met George Washington. The two were married the following January, in 1759. Unlike Martha's first husband, who was 20 years older, George was eight months her junior.

Martha and George Washington's wedding, 1759

M. Washington

> *I* have learned from experience that the greater part of our happiness or misery depends upon our dispositions, and not upon our circumstances.

George Washington's second inauguration in 1793

As the original first lady, Martha Washington knew she set the example for future presidential families. She was an active public figure, hosting events and helping care for military veterans. Every Friday and each New Year's Day, she also held receptions that were open to everyone, from government officials to local residents. These gatherings encouraged people to feel connected to their government, in opposition to the British traditions of royalty that the country left behind.

In letters, Washington expressed discomfort with the pressures in New York City (the first capital) and then in Philadelphia (the second capital). Yet she never presented this to the public, and she was known as a welcoming and charming person.

"*I* little thought, when the war was finished, that any circumstances could possibly have happened, which would call the General into public life again….Yet I cannot blame him, for having acted according to his ideas of duty, in obeying the voice of his country."

Martha Washington at Mount Vernon

Martha had four children with Daniel Parke Custis. Tragically, three of the children—Daniel, Frances, and Martha—died quite young. The fourth, John, had four children of his own. When John passed away, his children went to live with Martha and George Washington. The two youngest remained even after their mother remarried.

Martha travelled as George did. During the Revolutionary War (1775–1781), she stayed at encampments whenever possible. As first lady, she ran both the Mount Vernon household in Virginia and the presidential households in New York and Philadelphia. After George's second term as president, the family returned to the Mount Vernon plantation. A brief five years later, in 1802, Martha Washington died, just a few years after her husband.

The Washington family

> "You know me well enough, to do me the justice to believe, that I am only fond of what comes from the heart."

Mount Vernon, the Washington family home

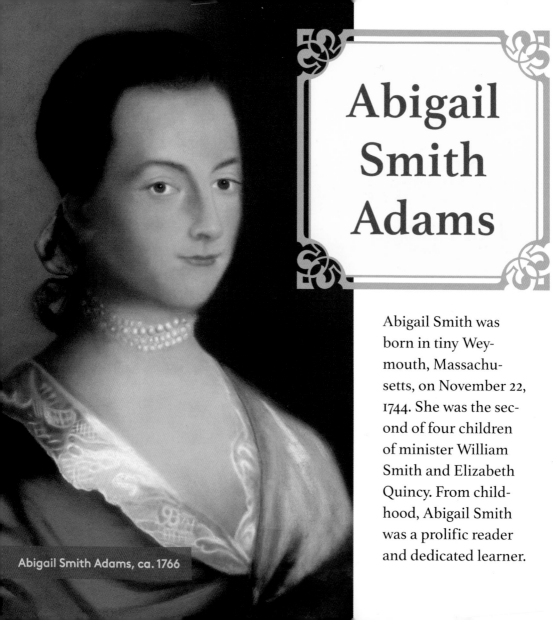

Abigail Smith Adams

Abigail Smith Adams, ca. 1766

Abigail Smith was born in tiny Weymouth, Massachusetts, on November 22, 1744. She was the second of four children of minister William Smith and Elizabeth Quincy. From childhood, Abigail Smith was a prolific reader and dedicated learner.

When she met up-and-coming lawyer John Adams, she found in him an easy companion in intellectual curiosity. The two married on October 25, 1764, and although Smith's father disapproved of John's limited prospects, he officiated the wedding himself.

Adams's childhood home

Abigail Adams

"Well, knowledge is a fine thing, and mother Eve thought so; but she smarted so severely for hers, that most of her daughters have been afraid of it since."

Abigail Adams was politically opinionated and outspoken about her views. As the Revolutionary War (1775–1783) brewed, she was a fervent supporter of independence. While spending time in French and British courts in the 1780s during John's time as a diplomat, she complained about the royalty and wrote of how much she preferred her chickens back home.

Adams did not start censoring herself once she became first lady in 1787, including when she disagreed with her husband. This was not the way Martha Washington had behaved. Adams' detractors said she had no right to be so political, as she not only was not an elected official, but was also a woman.

John Adams

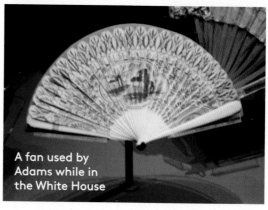

A fan used by Adams while in the White House

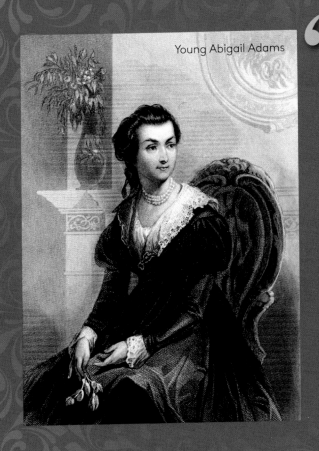

Young Abigail Adams

“*Do not put such unlimited power into the hands of the husbands. Remember all men would be tyrants if they could.*”

Abigail Adams in a portrait done during her time as first lady

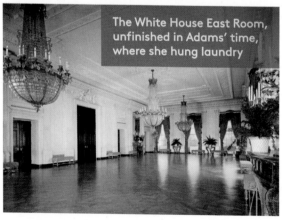
The White House East Room, unfinished in Adams' time, where she hung laundry

As first lady, Adams was a strong supporter of women's right to education, and she often spoke and wrote against the practice of enslavement. She also continued Martha Washington's tradition of hosting and socializing.

When the nation's capital moved from Philadelphia, Pennsylvania, to Washington, D.C., the Adamses became the first presidential couple to live in what would become the White House. The building, however, was still under construction. She wrote to family complaining about the rough, isolated conditions, but swore them to secrecy because she feared seeming ungrateful to the public.

> **"**If particular care and attention is not paid to the ladies, we are determined to foment a rebellion, and will not hold ourselves bound by any laws in which we have no voice or representation.**"**

Washington, D.C., in the early 1800s

The Adamses had six children, two of whom died young. But four lived to adulthood: Abigail (called "Nabby"), John Quincy (who later became president), Charles, and Thomas. The family's primary residence was a small farm in Braintree (now Quincy), Massachusetts. They also spent time in Boston, where John's law practice was located. Abigail Adams's talent for managing the children, farm, and finances is said to have kept the family going through hard times and good.

Much of the couple's marriage was spent apart, with John serving in the Continental Congress and later in diplomatic roles internationally. Throughout, Abigail and John regularly wrote each other long, heartfelt, witty, and detailed letters.

Adams died on October 28, 1818, less than seven years before her son John Quincy Adams was elected president.

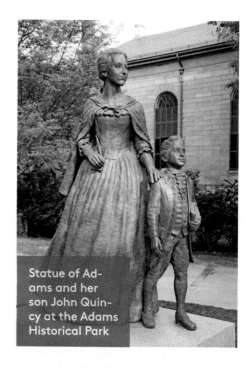

Statue of Adams and her son John Quincy at the Adams Historical Park

Tombs of Abigail and John Adams

The Adams family home in what is now Quincy, Massachusetts

> "No one is without difficulties, whether in high or low life, and every person knows best where their own shoe pinches."

Inside the Adams home in Massachusetts

Martha Jefferson Randolph

Martha Jefferson was born on September 27, 1772, the eldest child of Thomas Jefferson and his wife, Martha Wayles. Martha Jefferson's mother died when she was ten years old. Jefferson had one sister from her mother, and at least four half-siblings from her father and Sally Hemings, a woman who was enslaved in the Jefferson household.

Martha Jefferson Randolph, ca. 1805

Called "Patsy" while she was a child, Jefferson was intelligent, well educated, and socially adept. The Jefferson family had always been close with Thomas's third cousins the Randolphs, and Thomas Mann Randolph married Martha Jefferson in 1790.

Thomas Jefferson,
Martha Randolph's father

"Life is a checkered scene of light and shade. That clouds will sometimes arise in Boston as they did at Monticello to obscure the brightness of your day is certain, but let the experience of your past life remind you always, that it is but a passing evil, that a few hours perhaps and the scene will be restored to its pristine beauty."

As her father had no living wife, Martha Randolph took over many functions of first lady, primarily by managing the household and acting as hostess when needed. Randolph also managed her own household at the Edgehill plantation and Monticello, raising and educating her eleven children at the same time.

Randolph's husband was also a politician, serving variously as a Virginia congressman and as governor. Randolph and her children, however, spent most of their time at Monticello. The Randolphs' marriage was a rocky one, and they were estranged for many years. Randolph had to sell Monticello in 1827 to pay off growing debt. Still, when Randolph died on October 10, 1836, she was buried by her father and husband at Monticello.

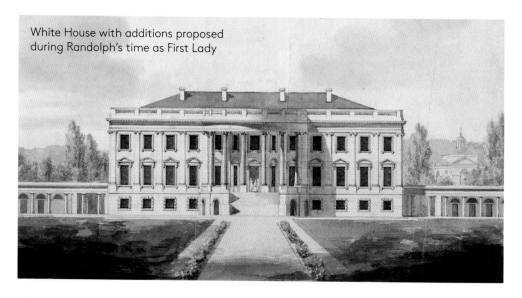

White House with additions proposed during Randolph's time as First Lady

> *I* am very fond of society but "toujours perdrix" [too much of a good thing] is insufferable.

Martha Randolph

Monticello

Dolley Payne Todd Madison

Dolley Payne was born on May 20, 1768, in North Carolina, one of eight children of John Payne and Mary Coles. The family were active Quakers, and eventually moved to Philadelphia, Pennsylvania, a center of Quaker society. While there, Dolley Payne

Dolley Madison, 1804

met John Todd, a young lawyer, and they married in 1790. The couple had two children, but a short three years into the marriage, Dolley lost her husband and the younger of her two sons to yellow fever.

The following year, Dolley Todd met the politician James Madison through Aaron Burr, a mutual friend. The two felt an immediate connection and married just four months later, on September 15, 1794. They moved into James Madison's plantation home in Montpelier, Virginia.

Young James Madison, ca. 1783

Miniature portrait of Madison, ca. 1805–1810

D. P. Madison

" *I* would rather fight with my hands than my tongue. "

The Madisons at a celebration of an American victory during the War of 1812

Dolley Madison was a legendarily skilled hostess, and her charm, wit, and social talents were invaluable to her as first lady. She even occasionally hosted events for Thomas Jefferson during his presidency, and helped raise funds for the Lewis and Clark expedition.

During her husband's presidency, Madison redecorated the presidential mansion (later called the White House) elegantly. She held regular receptions there that welcomed anyone who wanted to attend, be they working class or the social elite. She also made a practice of befriending other politicians and their wives, charming them into supporting her husband.

> " I am not afraid
> of anything. "

Madison, 1817

Gown worn by Madison as first lady

Madison's most memorable actions as first lady, however, took place during the War of 1812 (1812–1815). Soldiers were approaching the presidential home in the summer of 1814, and her husband was addressing issues elsewhere in the country. Madison helped organized the evacuation of valuable public artifacts, including government papers and the portrait of George Washington. She resisted evacuating herself as long as possible, hoping James would return before she left, but she ultimately had to go without him.

The White House showing fire and smoke damage after the attack in 1814

As British soldiers approached the presidential mansion, Madison wrote,

"*T*wo messengers covered with dust come bid me to fly, but I wait for him."

Madison organizing evacuation of the White House

Madison, 1848

The Madisons' marriage was affectionate. Dolley Madison's relationship to John Payne Todd, the surviving son from her first marriage, was tempestuous. Much of the family's wealth went toward paying of tens of thousands of dollars of debt that Todd had built up through gambling.

James Madison was often ill, especially late in his life. He died in 1836 at the family home of Montpelier. By this time, the plantation had suffered years of bad harvests and debt. In 1844, Dolley Madison sold the land; some of the people who had been enslaved there she sold to slave dealers, and others came under John Payne Todd's enslavement. Madison brought a few enslaved people with her to her smaller household in Washington, D.C. She lived there until her death on July 10, 1849.

The Madison family home in Montpelier, Virginia

"Habit and Hope are the crutches which support us through the vicissitudes of life."

Elizabeth Kortright Monroe

Elizabeth Kortright Monroe

Elizabeth Kortright was born on June 30, 1768, in New York City. Though her merchant father was wealthy at the time of her birth, he was staunchly loyal to the British crown. The family ended up losing most of their money during the Revolutionary War (1775–1783).

Elizabeth Kortright met James Monroe when she was just

sixteen years old. He was serving as a congressman from Virginia in the then-capital of New York City. They married a year later, on February 16, 1786, and moved to James's home in Fredricksburg, Virginia.

James Monroe

Elizabeth Monroe.

James Monroe said of his wife,

66 *I*t was improbable for any female to have fulfilled all the duties of the partner of such cares, and of a wife and parent, with more attention, delicacy and propriety than she has done. 99

Elizabeth Monroe generally travelled with her husband wherever his political career took him.

While James was ambassador to France during the country's civil war, Elizabeth saved the life of Adrienne de Lafayette, wife of the U.S. Revolutionary War hero the marquis de Lafayette. Adrienne was in prison awaiting the guillotine, but Monroe very publicly paid her a visit, and Lafayette was soon after released.

Adrienne de Lafayette

Monroe was immensely popular in France, but Americans tended to consider her European values elitist. Still, her style made a lasting impression on the White House. The building had been rebuilt after the War of 1812 (1812–1815), and Monroe furnished it in expensive, luxurious pieces primarily from Paris.

A journalist described Monroe in 1817 as,

An elegant, accomplished woman. She possesses a charming mind and dignity of manners.

Marquis de Lafayette

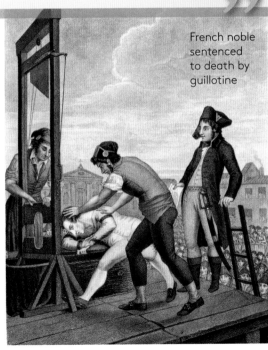

French noble sentenced to death by guillotine

The Monroes' marriage was a happy one, and their family was close. They had three children. One—the only son—died as an infant. Their two daughters, Eliza and Maria, spent their childhood travelling with their parents. Maria's wedding was held at the White House, an event that her mother chose to keep private. Eliza and her husband spent some time living there as well, and Eliza acted as hostess whenever her mother was ill.

After the end of James Monroe's second term as president, the couple returned to the family home and plantation in Virginia. Elizabeth died in Virginia on September 23, 1830, and her husband followed her less than a year later.

Highland (original building in white), one home of the Monroes, in Virginia

John Quincy Adams said that Monroe,

" *W*ith the external beauty and elegance of deportment, . . . united the more precious and endearing qualities which mark the fulfilment of all the social duties, and adorn with grace, and fill with enjoyment, the tender relations of domestic life. **"**

Eliza Monroe Hay, Monroe's daughter

Louisa Catherine Johnson Adams

Louisa Adams, early 1820s

Louisa Catherine Adams

Louisa Catherine Johnson was born on February 12, 1775, in London, England, to Maryland-born Joshua Johnson and British Catherine Nuth. Part of her childhood was spent in Nantes, France, but she primarily grew up in London. Johnson was an intelligent and curious student who loved science, music, and reading. She enjoyed a formal education until the 1780s, when her father's merchant business could no longer support it.

Joshua Johnson was the United States' first consul in London, and hosted many American diplomats working in Europe. The family hosted the minister to Netherlands, John Quincy Adams, in late 1795. Just six months after meeting her, John Quincy proposed to Louisa, but their wedding was delayed until July 1797 due to John's duties in the Netherlands.

John Quincy Adams, 1858

On first arriving in her husband's hometown of Quincy, Massachusetts, Adams wrote,

"Quincy! What shall I say of Quincy! Had I stepped into Noah's Ark I do-not think I could have been more utterly astonished."

During John Quincy's presidential campaign leading up to the 1824 election, Louisa Adams made up for her husband's social awkwardness with her own charm and grace. John Quincy won, but only barely, being placed in the role by the House of Representatives after a too-close election.

Louisa Adams then became the first foreign-born first lady, and the only one until 2017. Adams was often quite ill and generally resented the social requirements of her post, but she still fulfilled them with elegance. She held receptions, balls, and other events, sometimes playing music for her guests and often encouraging dancing. Both activities were highly unusual for the time.

A party in the Adamses' time in the White House

Adams once wrote of the White House,

Louisa Adams as first lady

" *T*here is something in this great unsocial house which depresses my spirits beyond expression and makes it impossible for me to feel at home or to fancy that I have a home any where. "

The Adamses had three healthy sons—George Washington, John, and Charles—and one daughter, Louisa Catherine, who died in her infancy. Adams supported her husband's political career, travelling

The Adams home in Massachusetts

across Europe and the United States as his duties demanded, taking their children with her whenever possible.

After John Quincy lost the election of 1828, the Adamses remained in Washington, D.C., while John Quincy served in Congress. Louisa Adams became heavily involved in her husband's efforts against slavery. The post-presidential years were difficult, however, as one son died in an apparent suicide in 1829, and another died of alcoholism in 1834. After Adams lost her husband in 1848, she became less active, and died just four years later, on May 15, 1852, in Washington, D.C.

Louisa Adams,
ca. 1835–1850

"*W*ith such
a husband and
such Son's I may
raise my head
with thankfulness
to my maker and
say 'Lord! now
let thy Servant
depart in peace
for I have been
greatly blessed.'"

John Quincy after his
unexpected collapse
in 1848

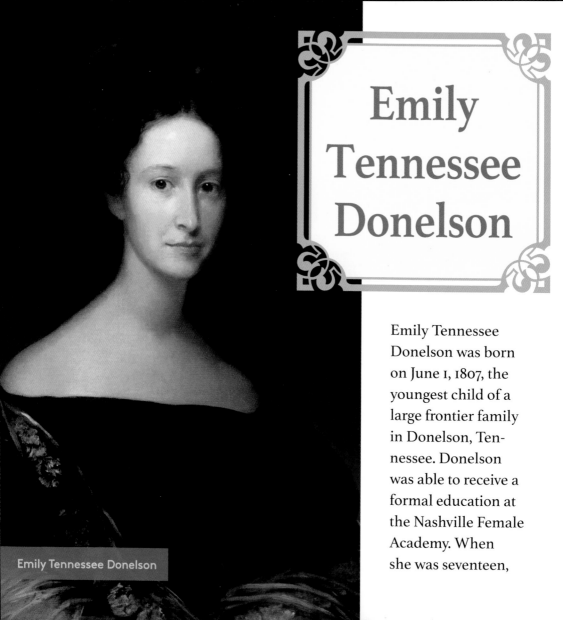

Emily Tennessee Donelson

Emily Tennessee Donelson

Emily Tennessee Donelson was born on June 1, 1807, the youngest child of a large frontier family in Donelson, Tennessee. Donelson was able to receive a formal education at the Nashville Female Academy. When she was seventeen,

Donelson married her cousin, Andrew Jackson Donelson. Andrew was a ward of Emily's aunt, Rachel Donelson Jackson, and Rachel's husband, Andrew Jackson.

Rachel Jackson died just months before her husband assumed the presidency in 1829. Now a widower, Jackson invited Donelson to the White House to act as first lady.

Rachel Jackson, Donelson's aunt

Andrew Jackson Donelson, Emily's husband

As first lady, Emily Donelson hosted balls, receptions, and other events. She was talented at it, and impressed guests with her charm and beauty. Donelson managed her growing family at the same time, having three of her four children while living at the White House.

Over the course of these years, Donelson and Jackson's relationship soured. The sticking point centered on Cabinet wife Peggy Eaton, whom Donelson snubbed due to rumors of affairs, and Jackson steadfastly defended. In 1834,

Jackson asked Donelson to leave the White House and brought in his daughter-in-law to replace her.

Donelson's health had already been declining, and this may have added to the reasons for her leaving the White House. When the family returned to Tennessee, her health worsened still. She died of tuberculosis in December 1836.

President Andrew Jackson

Angelica Singleton Van Buren

Angelica Singleton Van Buren

Angelica Singleton was born on February 13, 1818, to a wealthy plantation-owning family in South Carolina. As she grew up, Angelica made trips across Europe with her family and attended school in Nashville.

In 1838, Dolley Madison, a former first lady and distant

relative of the Singletons, invited Angelica to visit her in Washington, D.C. During the visit, Singleton and Madison had dinner with President Martin Van Buren and his four bachelor sons at the White House. Singleton experienced an immediate connection with the oldest son, Abraham, and the two were married that same year, on November 27. President Van Buren was a widower, and Abraham was the first of his sons to marry. As such, the new Mrs. Van Buren was a natural pick for first lady.

President Martin Van Buren

Angelica Van Buren leapt into the role of first lady, moving into the White House with her husband. She put her intelligence and charm to full use when she hosted events. Efforts to introduce some European-inspired manners and habits, however, offended many

The White House around the time of Van Buren's stay

Americans and reduced her popularity. Tragedy also marred her time at the White House. In 1840, Van Buren had a baby girl, Rebecca, who died shortly after being born. Van Buren herself suffered poor health for months after.

After leaving the White House in 1841, Angelica Van Buren and her husband lived between Kinderhook in New York and South Carolina, before eventually settling in New York City. The couple had three sons, and they raised one of Angelica's nieces alongside them. Angelica Van Buren died in New York on December 29, 1877.

A journalist wrote the
Van Buren was a

" *L*ady of rare ac-
complishments,
very modest yet
perfectly easy and
graceful in her
manners and free
and vivacious in
her conversation. "

Angelica Van Buren during
her time as first lady

Anna Tuthill Symmes Harrison

Anna Tuthill Symmes was born on July 25, 1775, in Morristown, New Jersey. Her mother died when Anna was one year old, and her father, a Continental soldier, dressed in a British uniform to smuggle his young daughter across enemy-controlled New York

Anna Tuthill Symmes Harrison

state to his parents-in-law. Anna remained with her grandparents until her father remarried and was able to care for her properly.

Anna Symmes enjoyed an excellent education until moving with her father to the Ohio frontier in 1795. That same year, she met William Henry Harrison, then a soldier at a nearby garrison. Anna's father disapproved of Harrison, so the two married in secret on November 25, 1795. Over the next nineteen years, the happy couple had ten children, only one of whom outlived Anna.

William Henry Harrison, ca. 1813

They had retired to a farm at North Bend, Ohio, when Anna's husband was asked to run for president in 1840. Despite Anna's resistance, he agreed and won a landslide victory.

Anna Harrison was ill and did not attend the inauguration the following March. She was packing her things to join her husband in April, just four weeks after he became president, when she received word of his death from pneumonia. She was the first first lady to be widowed while holding the title.

Congress granted Anna Harrison a pension, and she lived the rest of her life in Ohio. She died on February 25, 1864.

President Harrison, 1840

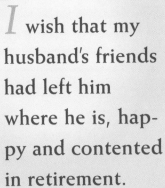

Anna Harrison

William Henry Harrison Tomb State Memorial, where both Anna and William are burried

" *I* wish that my husband's friends had left him where he is, happy and contented in retirement. "

Letitia Christian Tyler, before her time in the White House

Letitia Christian Tyler

Letitia Christian was born on November 12, 1790, to a plantation-owning family in Virginia. Christian was the seventh of twelve children. Little is known of her childhood, beyond that she learned the skills of managing a household, family, and plantation.

John Tyler once told his daughter that,

"*He* rarely failed to consult her [Letitia Tyler's] judgment in the midst of difficulties and troubles, and that she invariably led him to the best conclusion."

Christian met John Tyler when they were both young, as Tyler grew up not far from the Christian family. They married on March 29, 1813, and eventually had eight children, one of whom died young.

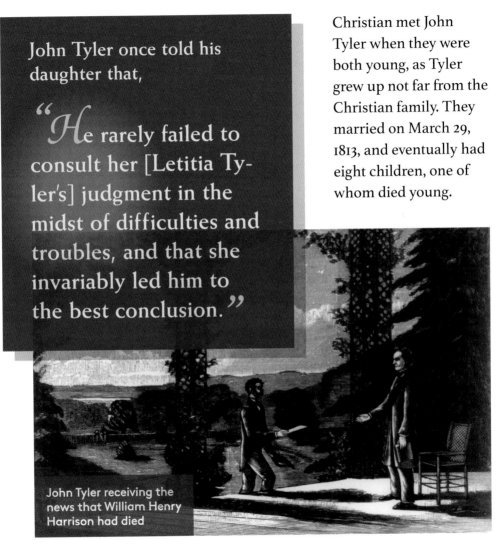

John Tyler receiving the news that William Henry Harrison had died

Letitia Tyler stayed behind the scenes throughout her husband's political career, managing the children, finances, and household. Even after she suffered a severe stroke that left her mostly paralyzed, she continued to make sure everything with the family ran smoothly. Nothing changed when she unexpectedly became first lady in 1841, following the death of President William Henry Harrison. While two daughters and a daughter-in-law took care of hosting parties and receptions, Tyler took care of everything else from her private chambers in the White House. She did, however, attend the wedding when her daughter Elizabeth was married at the White House.

In 1842, Tyler suffered a second stroke that lead to her death soon after, on September 10, 1842.

Letitia's daughter and namesake, Letitia Tyler Semple, sometimes acted as White House hostess. Letitia became estranged from her father when he remarried after her mother's death.

Tyler's daughter-in-law Priscilla Cooper Tyler said of her,

"**M**other attends to and regulates all the household affairs and all so quietly that you can't tell when she does it."

John and Letitia's son Robert married actress Priscilla Cooper, a vivacious woman who charmed visitors to the White House when she acted as White House hostess.

Julia Gardiner Tyler

Julia Gardiner was born on May 4, 1820, on the family-owned Gardiners Island, New York. Her family was part of the social elite of New York, and she grew up attending finishing school and touring Europe.

Gardiner met John Tyler in 1841 while her family wintered in Washington, D.C.

An oil painting created between 1846 and 1848

Tyler proposed to her in February 1843, five months after the death of his first wife. Gardiner's parents disapproved, however, because he was a full 30 years older than she. After the unexpected death of Gardiner's father during a visit to a naval ship with the president in 1844, Tyler proposed again. The two became engaged in secret and married in a private ceremony on June 26, 1844.

> After I lost my father, I felt differently toward the President. He seemed…to be more agreeable…than any younger man.

A dress worn by Julia during her time in the White House

In her eight months as first lady, Julia Tyler brought opulent, elegant, formal receptions and celebrations to the White House. Guests were charmed by her, and those who did not attend events were still able to admire her activities thanks to the agent she hired to improve her press coverage. She may have left a lasting mark on White House events, as some reports say she was the first to have "Hail to the Chief" played when the president entered.

Tyler was also an active participant in politics, a marked change from many first ladies before her. She lobbied successfully for Texas to become a state in 1845. She was also an open supporter of enslavement, and even aligned herself with the Confederacy later, during the Civil War (1861–1865).

> *"Nothing appears to delight the President more than…to hear people sing my praises."*

The Tylers were married at the Church of the Ascension in New York. Only one of John's sons knew about and attended the wedding.

The Tylers had seven children together. It was a large family, with fifteen children in all, including those John had with his first wife. They settled at the Tyler plantation near Richmond, Virginia, after leaving the White House. A habit of overspending, however, drained the Tylers' finances. When John Tyler died in 1863, Julia left their Virginia plantation to move in with her mother in Long Island, New York. By the end of the war in 1865, Julia was largely penniless, and she started lobbying for a pension as a presidential widow. She survived on this financial help until her death on July 10, 1889, in Virginia.

Lyon Gardiner Tyler, one of Julia's sons, was named after her ancestor Lion Gardiner who had purchased the family island.

John and Julia Gardiner Tyler are buried at Hollywood Cemetery in Richmond, Virginia.

The Tyler plantation was named Sherwood Forest by John. The House remains in the Tyler family.

Tyler wrote in a poem to her husband,

" *W*hat e'er changes time may bring, I'll love thee as thou art! "

A print created in 1846, during Polk's presidency

Sarah Childress Polk

Sarah Childress was born on September 4, 1803, to a plantation-owning family in Murfreesboro, Tennessee. She grew up highly educated, with private tutors, school attendance in Nashville, and a place at the Moravian Female Academy in Salem, North Carolina.

Childress knew the young clerk James Polk from local social events. At the suggestion of Andrew Jackson, a politician on the rise and a mutual acquaintance, Polk proposed to Childress. She agreed to marry him, but only after he won a political office. Polk won a seat on the Tennessee state legislature in 1823. The following January 1, the two were married at the Childress family home.

This lithograph was likely created in 1838. At the time, James Polk was a member of the U.S. House of Representatives and had ascended to become Speakevr of the House.

Sarah Polk cared more about politics than she did about housekeeping. As first lady, she was an active adviser for her husband and dealt equally with his political friends and foes. She made few cosmetic changes to the White House, but did install gas lighting.

As a hostess, Polk was subdued but generous. Very religious, she never drank or danced, and forbid both to anyone at the White House on Sundays. But she was friendly, intelligent, and an adept conversationalist, and guests almost universally liked her.

This painting by George Dury was modeled after an earlier painting by George Healy.

Polk kept costs down by not having paid household staff. Instead, she took care of secretarial duties for her husband; enslaved people from the Polk plantation had to cover the rest of the work. Though she was far from the first person to use enslaved labor at the White House, she was the first to use it to replace paid labor entirely.

A photograph of the White House taken 1846, during the Polk presidency

> *I*f I should be so fortunate as to reach the White House,…I will neither keep house nor make butter.

James Polk's inauguration was a rainy affair.

The Polks had no children. Sarah instead invested most of her time supporting her husband in his political endeavors, helping shape both his politics and his career. When she was unable to travel with him on his campaigns, she kept him informed of local opinions and events by mail.

Life together ended when James died, barely three months after leaving office in 1849. Sarah Polk remained at their home of Polk Place in Nashville, Tennessee, for the remainder of her life, and never remarried. She died on August 14, 1891.

Sarah Polk wrote a letter to the local newspaper in support of her husband's pursuit of expansionism and the idea of Manifest Destiny. The Polk presidency saw the country grow larger in the aftermath of the Mexican-American War.

James Polk's final words to his wife were reportedly,

"*I* love you Sarah.
For all eternity, I love you."

James and Sarah Polk are now buried on the grounds at the Tennessee State Capitol.

Margaret "Peggy" Mackall Smith Taylor

Photographs of Margaret are few. This is one of two known photographs.

Margaret Mackall Smith was born to a Maryland plantation family on September 2, 1788, the youngest of seven children. Little is known of her childhood, though it is clear she had a genteel upbringing among some of America's social elite. By the time she was sixteen years old, Smith had lost both her parents, and moved to Louisville, Kentucky, to live with an older sister. She met the young army officer Zachary Taylor there in 1809. They married June 21, 1810. In the following decades, the couple moved across the frontier, following Zachary Taylor's postings and living in all manners of conditions. They had six children, though two died quite young.

Zachary Taylor once stated,

" *My* wife was as much of a soldier as I was. "

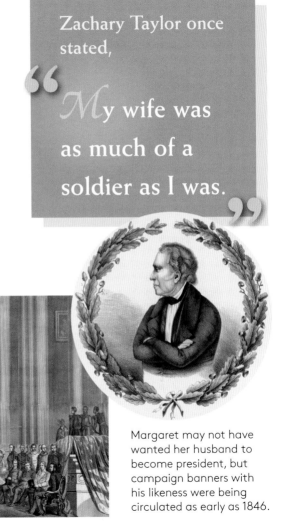

A contemporary illustration shows Zachary Taylor's inauguration.

Margaret may not have wanted her husband to become president, but campaign banners with his likeness were being circulated as early as 1846.

Margaret Taylor entered the White House reluctantly in 1848. Taylor generally managed the household and took visitors in her private quarters, leaving each day to attend church services but rarely for another reason. Social responsibilities were covered her daughter Betty Taylor Bliss. Taylor's lack of interest in the social side of first ladyship is reportedly because, during her husband's time in the military, she made a vow to give up all "frivolity" if her husband remained safe.

When Zachary Taylor unexpectedly died of gastroenteritis in July 1850, Margaret was devastated. After leaving Washington, she stayed at the homes of her children until dying barely two years after her husband, on August 14, 1852.

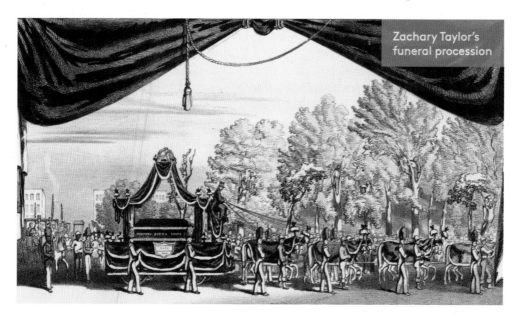

Zachary Taylor's funeral procession

The couple are buried at Zachary Taylor National Cemetery in Louisville, Kentucky.

As a young man Jefferson Davis, later president of the Confederacy, was briefly married to the Taylors' daughter Sarah. Sarah died only a few months into the marriage of malaria, causing Margaret and Zachary great grief.

Abigail Powers Fillmore

A lifelong reader, Abigail hosted Charles Dickens and Washington Irving while she was in the White House.

Abigail Powers was born on March 13, 1798, in Stillwater, New York, the youngest of seven children. The family had little extra money, but her father, Baptist minister Lemuel Powers, had built up a large personal library, and both parents highly valued education. Abigail was an avid reader

and learner, and she was teaching at a small school in New Hope, New York, by the age of sixteen.

It was at the school that Powers later met Millard Fillmore. At nineteen, he was the oldest of Powers' students and two years younger than she. The two immediately connected over a love of books and learning. After a long courtship, the two were married on February 5, 1826.

Abigail Fillmore

Millard Fillmore ran as the Whig candidate for vice president in 1848.

Abigail's dress in the First Ladies collection at the Smithsonian

When Millard became vice president under Zachary Taylor in 1849, Abigail stayed at home in Buffalo, New York. The whole family moved into the White House when Taylor died, making Millard Fillmore president. Abigail became the first of any first lady to have held a job outside the home.

Abigail Fillmore preferred books to balls and often suffered ill health, so she sometimes left the role of hostess to her daughter Mary. Abigail, however, was very active outside the big social gatherings. Disappointed to find the White House lacked any library, she built one. She also started holding cultural and educational events. Politically active, she regularly shared ideas and advice with her husband, including that he should veto the unpopular Fugitive Slave Bill in 1850.

Fillmore said of selecting books for the White House library, "*I* do not recollect when I had such a mental treat."

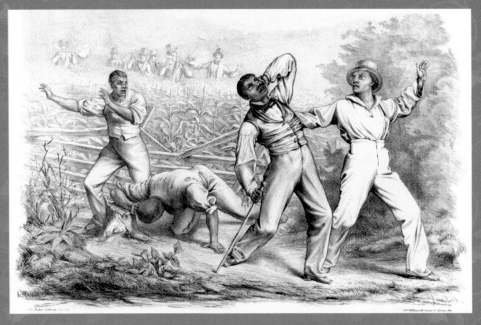

The Fugitive Slave Law, which required that authorities in free states were required to track down enslaved people who had escaped, was unpopular in the North. Fillmore did not receive his party's nomination to run for the presidency in 1852 partly because he lost many of his party's Northern supporters by signing it.

The Fillmores had two children: Millard Jr., and Mary Abigail. Abigail Fillmore stopped teaching professionally when her children were born, and switched to taking care of the household and teaching her children. She kept up an active intellectual life, however, and cultivated friendships with people who also valued learning.

Fillmore was often ill or in pain as first lady, and her health was rapidly declining as her husband's presidency came to an end. Despite this,

Daughter Mary Abigail, also known as Abbie, frequently served as White House hostess in her mother's stead.

she attended the inauguration for the next president, Franklin Pierce, where she caught a cold. That cold ultimately proved fatal, and Fillmore died on March 30, 1853, just weeks after leaving the White House.

Franklin Pierce's inaugural event proved deadly for Abigail.

Jane Means Appleton Pierce

Jane Means Appleton was born on March 12, 1806, in Hampton, New Hampshire, the third of six children. Growing up, Jane came to love literature and music, and even studied music for a time in Boston, Massachusetts.

Appleton met Franklin Pierce when he was a student at

An engraving of Jane Pierce

Eng. by J. C. Buttre

Bowdoin College. Appleton's father had been president of Bowdoin before his death in 1819, and her sister was married to a professor there, so Jane often spent time around people associated with the school. Pierce quickly fell for her, and though Appleton disliked politics and her family disapproved of the match, he eventually won them all over. The couple married on November 19, 1834.

Franklin Pierce circa 1852. Pierce was a brigadier general in the Mexican-American War.

The couple likely met through their connections at Bowdoin College.

Jane Pierce was never a fan of politics or the vast amount of socializing that came with being a politician's wife. This dislike deepened when her last surviving son, Bennie, died in a train accident at the age of eleven, just a few weeks before Franklin's inauguration.

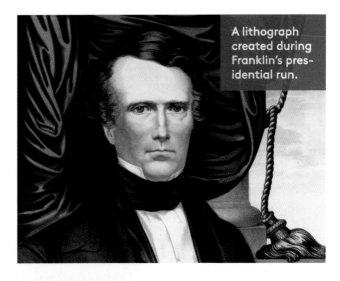

A lithograph created during Franklin's presidential run.

Jane with her son Bennie

During her time in the White House, Pierce struggled with deep depression and a suffocating grief. She generally lacked the energy or interest needed for managing the household or hosting events, and relatives often acted as hostess in her place.

When he heard Franklin would run for president, Bennie wrote his mother,

" *I* hope he won't be elected for I should not like to be at Washington and I know you would not either. "

An illustration shows Franklin Pierce leaving a hotel to attend his inauguration.

Pierce Manse in Concord, New Hampshire, was Jane and Franklin's home between 1842 and 1848, during Franklin's hiatus from politics.

Jane Pierce's resentment of and her husband's devotion to his political career made for an often-unhappy marriage. She successfully convinced Franklin to resign from his Senate seat in 1842, but he broke his promise to stay out of politics when he ran for president ten years later.

The couple had three sons, all of whom died young. The first, Franklin Jr., passed away in 1836 when he was just three days old. The second, named Frank Robert, was born in 1839 and died just four years later. Benjamin, called "Bennie," lived to be eleven.

After the presidency, the Pierces travelled to Europe to hopefully improve Jane's health, but to no avail. She died on December 2, 1863, in Massachusetts.

> *Oh* how I wish he was out of political life! How much better it would be for him on every account!

The Pierce family gravesite is found in New Hampshire.

Harriet Rebecca Lane Johnston

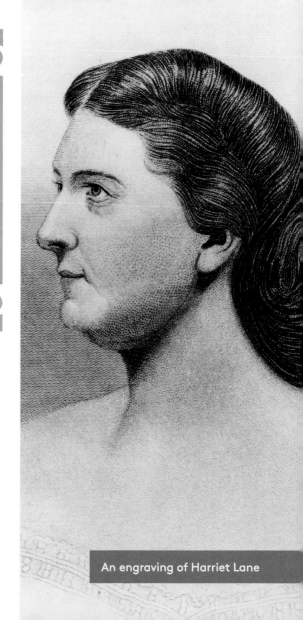

Harriet Rebecca Lane was born on May 9, 1830, the youngest child in a wealthy family of Mercersburg, Pennsylvania. Her mother died when she was nine years old, and her father followed two years later. As a result, Lane and her sister came under the guardianship of "Nunc," Lane's favorite uncle, politician James Buchanan.

An engraving of Harriet Lane

Buchanan sent the sisters to boarding schools and an academy in Washington, D.C. He also educated them himself on issues of politics. Harriet Lane had a particular flair for politics, and she joined her uncle in London while he was minister of Great Britain. When Buchanan—a lifelong bachelor—was elected president in 1856, he asked Harriet to act as his first lady.

Harriet Lane charmed Queen Victoria, shown here, during her time in Great Britain. Queen Victoria wanted her to accept a marriage proposal from Sir Fitzroy Kelly so that she would stay in the country.

Harriet Lane

"**Without doubt, our people are more prompt and eloquent.** "

Harriet enjoyed her time in London; she did, however, think that speeches in the United States were better.

One of Harriet Lane's dresses is included in the Smithsonian's First Ladies collection.

This engraving of James Buchanan was completed ca. 1860.

Harriet Lane was an active and highly adept first lady. Serving during the contentious years leading up to the Civil War (1861–1865), she carefully laid out complex seating arrangements that kept people separate from their enemies and treated everyone equitably. This, combined with her charm, intelligence, tact, and beauty, made her incredibly popular among politicians and civilians alike.

Lane worked on many projects as first lady, and she was a regular adviser for Buchanan. One prominent example is her advocacy for Native Americans. She lobbied successfully to improve living conditions on reservations and worked to make sure lawmakers were well versed in the individual needs of various tribes. She also supported the arts, often inviting artists to the White House.

"**T**hink of my feelings when the lovely lac-quered boxes and tables from the Japanese Embassy brought me were turned from the door."

James Buchanan didn't permit his niece to accept any gifts from visitors to the White House, a source of playful frustration.

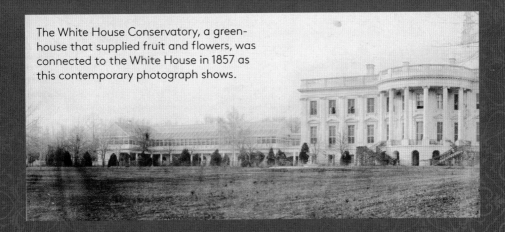

The White House Conservatory, a green-house that supplied fruit and flowers, was connected to the White House in 1857 as this contemporary photograph shows.

Harriet Lane Johnston was a benefactor of what would become the Smithsonian Institution's National Gallery of Art.

Lane had plenty of suitors but chose not to marry until after leaving the White House. As a single woman, she helped her uncle with his political career. After a trip to Europe, she also started what would become an impressive art collection, which she eventually donated to the National Gallery of Art at the Smithsonian Institution.

When she was 36 years old, Lane married banker Henry Elliot Johnston, with whom she settled in Washington, D.C. They had two sons together, but both died in their teens. Henry Johnston followed before the couple had reached their twentieth anniversary. Harriet herself died on July 3, 1903. Her will included a large donation that created what is now the Harriet Lane Clinic, a pediatric facility at Johns Hopkins.

Lane once described her suitors as

"*P*leasant but dreadfully troublesome."

Harriet Lane was the namesake of several Coast Guard ships, including this one, the USRC *Harriet Lane* commissioned in 1857.

Mary Todd Lincoln

This photograph was taken by renowned Civil War photographer Mathew Brady.

In 1818, Mary Todd was born in Lexington, Kentucky, the fourth of seven children of wealthy banker and slaveowner Robert Smith Todd and his wife Elizabeth. Mary knew grief early: her mother died when she was six. Robert remarried, and he and Elizabeth Humphreys had nine children together. Mary's relationship with her stepmother was contentious.

Mary was living with one of her sisters in Springfield, Illinois, when she met Abraham Lincoln. (Lincoln's debate opponent Stephen Douglas was also a prospective suitor.) Although Abraham broke off their first engagement, they came together again and married in 1842.

Mary Lincoln

Mary Todd's childhood home in Lexington, Kentucky

> "*C*louds and darkness surround us, yet Heaven is just, and the day of triumph will surely come, when justice and truth will be vindicated. Our wrongs will be made right, and we will once more taste the blessings of freedom, of which the degraded rebels would deprive us."
>
> Letter, 1861

Lincoln had an intense interest in politics and encouraged her husband's political ambitions, writing letters on his behalf and cultivating allies. However, she found her time in the White House difficult. Siblings and half-siblings fought on both sides of the war, and she was sometimes perceived as a traitor by both sides, though she was known for volunteering at Union hospitals and visiting troops. Her son Willie died of typhoid fever in 1862 at the age of eleven. Lincoln also dealt with a great deal of criticism for her spending. Her mental health suffered—historians later speculated that she might have had bipolar disorder—and after a carriage accident in 1863 in which she hit her head, her lifelong migraines grew even more frequent.

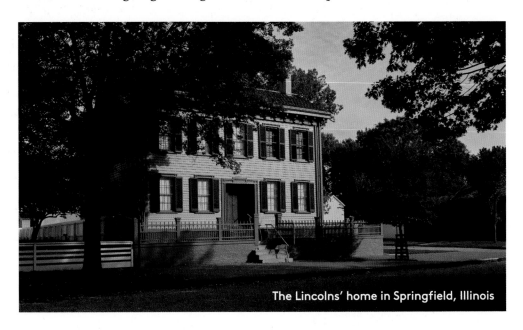

The Lincolns' home in Springfield, Illinois

The Lincoln family with sons Robert Todd and Tad. A painting on the wall shows Willie, their deceased son.

66

I must dress in costly materials. The people scrutinize every article that I wear with critical curiosity. The very fact of having grown up in the West, subjects me to more searching observation. 99

As quoted by Elizabeth Keckley, a former enslaved woman who was Mary's dressmaker and confidante, in her memoir *Behind the Scenes*

Peterson House, where Abraham Lincoln was taken after he was shot. Mary and her son waited in this front parlor for news.

Mary Todd Lincoln was present when her husband was shot in April 1865. He was taken to the home of a nearby tailor, William Peterson, where Mary waited in the parlor with their son Robert until shortly before his death, when she said her goodbyes. Distraught, she returned to Illinois.

Abraham Lincoln was the first president to be assassinated in office. Mary lobbied for a widow's pension. Congress voted narrowly to approve it, but Mary developed a fear that she would be left in poverty.

> "*I*ll luck presided at my birth— certainly within the last few years it has been a faithful attendant."

Mary Todd Lincoln is pictured here in black mourning attire after Abraham's death.

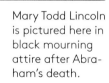

A depiction of Lincoln's death

Robert Lincoln

Mary and Abraham Lincoln had four children. Robert, born 1843, was the only of their children to outlive Mary. (He later served as Secretary of War to James Garfield and Chester Arthur.) Edward, born in 1846, died at the age of 3. William, or Willie, was born in 1850 and died during Lincoln's presidency. Thomas, or Tad, was born in 1853. When he died in 1871 at the age of 18, it was another grave blow to Mary.

In 1875, her mental health deteriorated to the extent that her son Robert had her institutionalized. She enlisted friends to argue on her behalf that she did not need to stay at the sanitorium and was released. She spent time in Europe before returning to her sister's Springfield home, where she died in 1882.

A painting of the Lincoln family

" I am allowed tranquility here.

Letter written by Mary in Europe

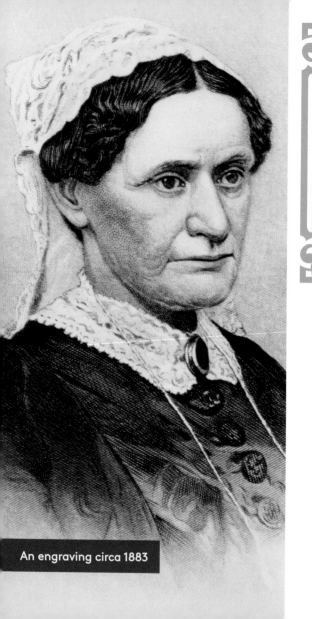

An engraving circa 1883

Eliza McCardle Johnson

A Tennessee native, Eliza McCardle was born to John McCardle and Sarah Phillipps on October 4, 1810. Eliza's father, a shoemaker and innkeeper, died in 1826 when she was only a teenager. That same year, at the age of sixteen, Eliza met her future husband, Andrew Johnson, a few years old than she. The young couple married a year later, in 1827.

The two lived together in Greeneville, Tennessee, with Andrew working first as a tailor. Eliza had been well-educated at Rhea Academy, and she helped her husband hone his speaking skills, encouraging him to join a debate society. She was his companion as he built his political career, from alderman to mayor to congressman to governor to senator.

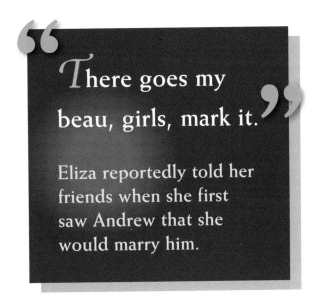

"There goes my beau, girls, mark it."

Eliza reportedly told her friends when she first saw Andrew that she would marry him.

Eliza Johnson

The house in Greeneville is now a National Historic Site.

Andrew Johnson, the only Southern senator to stay loyal to the Union, was named vice president in 1865. He was only in that role for a month before Lincoln's assassination elevated him to the presidency. Eliza had remained in Tennessee, although she had to evacuate to Nashville under harrowing circumstances when her home was confiscated for use by Confederate soldiers. She joined her husband at the White House when he became president, but she was suffering from tuberculosis and lived quietly. Her daughter, Martha Patterson, often acted as hostess in her stead.

The sergeant-at-arms serves the notice of impeachment to President Johnson.

When Johnson became the first president to be impeached, Eliza acted as his advisor. Although she did not attend the trial in person, she followed it keenly. She also played a part in directing updates to parts of the White House that needed refurbishment.

Martha Johnson Patterson, Johnson's daughter and frequent White House hostess

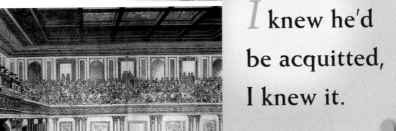

The impeachment trial

"*I* knew he'd be acquitted, I knew it."

Andrew Johnson National Historic Site in Greeneville, Tennessee

Eliza and Andrew had five children: daughters Martha and Mary, and sons Charles, Robert, and Andrew Jr. Tragically, Eliza was predeceased by two of her children. Charles, a doctor who joined the Union Army as an assistant surgeon, died when he was thrown from a horse in 1863. Robert suffered from alcoholism and committed suicide in 1869.

Throughout their marriage, Eliza managed the family home and finances. The family relied on the labor of enslaved people, including Sam, Dolly, and Henry, who were freed in 1863.

Early in her husband's career, Eliza would reportedly attend local rallies, and she would sometimes visit Washington, D.C., when he was a representative. As her health declined, she could do less. Post-presidency, the family returned home to Greeneville. Andrew died in 1875, and Eliza followed six months later, in January, 1876.

The Johnson family plot at Andrew Johnson National Cemetery

> " *S*he was the stepping stone to all the honors and fame my father attained. "

Martha Patterson, writing of her mother

Photographs of Julia Dent Grant generally show her in profile. She was self-conscious about her strabismus (crossed eyes).

Julia Dent Grant

Julia Boggs Dent was born in 1826 in Missouri to Frederick Dent and Ellen Wrenshall Dent. One of eight children, Julia was raised at a plantation worked by about 30 enslaved persons. In a later memoir, Julia described her childhood as happy. Their family had a wide social circle that included explorer William Clark and other local luminaries, and Julia was well-educated at an elite boarding school. She enjoyed reading poetry and literary works.

Julia was introduced to Ulysses through her brother, Frederick Jr., after the two men met at West Point. Their affection for each other did not wane while Grant was serving in the Mexican-American War, and they wrote frequently. They married in 1848, on his return from the war.

Julia D Grant

At a reception in 1865, President Lincoln welcomes Julia Grant to the White House. Julia and Mary Todd Lincoln reportedly did not like each other.

> "You can have but little idea of the influence you have over me Julia, even while so far away... and thus it is absent or present I am more or less governed by what I think is your will."

Ulysses Grant, in a letter to Julia

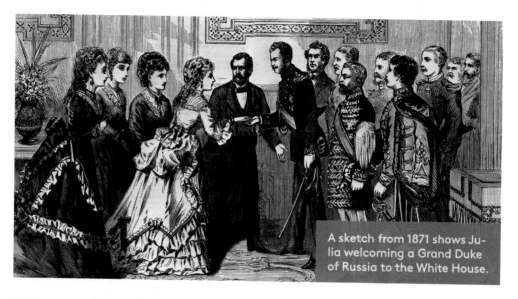

A sketch from 1871 shows Julia welcoming a Grand Duke of Russia to the White House.

Julia was ambitious for her husband and delighted when he won the presidency; she would have wished for him to run for a third term. She was an active first lady, entertaining often and enjoying lavish formal dinners. Her time in the White House saw the refurbishment of some family rooms, some executive offices, and some public rooms. Her daughter Nellie was married in the redecorated East Room.

Accusations of scandal and nepotism plagued her husband's presidency, and the appointment of several of Julia's relatives did not help. Julia garnered both praise and criticism from the press. In speaking to the press frequently, and in raising the profile of her marriage and children, she helped shape the ideal of a "first family."

"**W**hy, you are getting to be such a great man, and I am such a plain little wife. I thought if my eyes were as others are I might not be so very, very plain."

"**D**id I not see you and fall in love with you with these same eyes?"

An exchange between Julia and Ulysses after he became president, as recounted in her memoirs

Nellie Grant's wedding at the White House was a sumptuous affair.

Julia and Ulysses had four children: Frederick Dent Grant, Ulysses Simpson Grant, Ellen "Nellie" Grant, and Jesse Root Grant. The couple were devoted to each other and affectionate with each other, writing voluminously when separated. During the Civil War (1861–1865), Julia often stayed with Ulysses during campaigns, and her presence was seen as providing a steadying influence that helped propel his success.

After the presidency, the couple traveled around the world. They suffered from financial woes, however, on their return, and Ulysses was diagnosed with throat cancer. He wrote his memoirs as he was dying to gain money. The widowed Julia wrote her own memoir, though it was not published until long after her death. She died in 1902.

Julia is shown here with her father Frederick, son Jesse, and daughter Nellie.

Julia Grant in a post-presidency photograph. She sits next to her son, soldier Frederick Dent Grant.

Julia was buried alongside her husband in Grant's Tomb.

> " *A* panacea for loneliness, a tonic for old age. "

Grant on the process of writing her memoir,
a pursuit she found absorbing and rewarding

This photograph of Hayes was taken in the 1860s.

Lucy Webb Hayes

Lucy Webb was born in 1831 in Ohio to Dr. James Webb and Maria Cook, the youngest of three. The family was Methodist and leaned towards abolition. Lucy's father died when she was a toddler; he had gone to his family home to free enslaved people he had inherited and caught cholera. Lucy's mother and paternal grandfather, Isaac Webb, raised Lucy and her brothers to believe

Lucy W. Hayes.

that slavery was wrong. Isaac Webb was also a staunch proponent of the temperance movement and would pass along that belief to his granddaughter.

Lucy attended Cincinnati Wesleyan Female College and was the first first lady to receive a college degree. She and Rutherford Hayes first met when Lucy was 14, and then again when she was older. They married in 1852.

> "My greatest happiness now would be to feel that I was doing some thing for the comfort and happiness of our men I feel that in giving you up—(for dearest it is hard to feel we may be parted) I have tried to do cheerfully and without a murmur what was my duty."
>
> Letter written during the Civil War to Rutherford Hayes in 1861

The Hayes family entered the White House under clouded circumstances. Hayes was not declared the winner until five months and a lot of behind-the-scenes maneuvering and negotiations had passed. Nonetheless, Lucy's tenure in the White House had several notable moments. She was likely the first to be called "First Lady" as a title. Bathrooms with running water were installed during the Hayes administration, as was the first telephone. The first White House Easter Egg Roll also took place un-

A dress worn by Hayes in her time at the White House

der her auspices, when children were banned from the Capitol grounds.

While Lucy was popular for her charitable work and hosting, she later was the subject of some criticism. The Hayes administration was generally a dry one, ultimately at Rutherford's direction, but it was Lucy who was blamed after her death and dubbed "Lemonade Lucy."

Marie Selika Williams, the first Black musician to perform at the White House. She did so at Hayes's request.

> " *F*rom such great joy how soon we were filled with sorrow and grief past utterance I do not know how you will feel—whether Mercy or Justice—will be nearest your heart. "

Lucy wrote to her husband on April 17, 1865. President Lincoln had been assassinated on April 15, less than a week after the Confederate surrender at Appomattox.

Lucy Hayes with her husband President Rutherford Hayes

Lucy was the mother of eight, with the first child born in 1856 and the last born in 1873. Three of her children—Joseph, George, and Manning—died when they were very young.

Rutherford served in the Civil War, and Lucy spent some time with him at the front, aiding not only him but other soldiers in his regiment. She was actively engaged in her husband's politics, listening to Congressional debates, traveling with him, and visiting prisons and hospitals during his tenure as governor. When the couple returned to Ohio, she continued with various charitable works and reform efforts before her death at the age of 57 in 1889.

"My life with you has been so happy—so successful—so beyond reasonable anticipations, that I think of you with a loving gratitude that I do not know how to express."

Rutherford Hayes in a letter written to Lucy in 1870

Lucretia Rudolph Garfield

Born Lucretia Rudolph in 1832, "Crete" was the eldest daughter of farmer and carpenter Zebulon Rudolph and Arabella Mason. Her parents were earnest believers in education, and Lucretia was a good student with a gift for public speaking. She first met James Garfield at school in 1849, but they did not immediately fall in love.

Their paths later crossed again in college; in fact, star student Garfield briefly taught Lucretia in her Greek class when the teacher became ill. After graduation, Lucretia became a teacher. After a long courtship and correspondence, Lucretia and James eventually married in 1858.

James Garfield as a teenager

" *T*rue, it has become almost a proverb that when a lady is married, she may as well lay aside her books; still I do not believe it contains very much wisdom after all; and even if it did, you know my superior powers would warrant me in being the exception. I trust you will pardon my nonsense. "

Letter from Lucretia to James, 1854

The Garfield family

Lucretia's time in the White House was extremely brief. She advised her husband on some of his cabinet appointments and immersed herself in studies of the history of the White House. However, she was struck by malaria in May. She was at the seaside recovering from malaria when her husband was shot by an assassin in July. She returned immediately to Washington, D.C. Garfield spent the next several months fighting for his life before he died. The family left Washington, D.C., to return to Ohio shortly after.

A newspaper illustration at the time

Oh, why am I made to suffer this cruel wrong?
Reportedly said by Lucretia at James's passing

Garfield was the mother of seven, five surviving to adulthood. The couple were active in the Washington, D.C., social circle when James was a congressman, and avid reader Lucretia joined a literary society. After her husband's death, Lucretia raised their children (the youngest was only 8). She also, in honor of her husband, organized and preserved her husband's papers, a forerunner of today's modern presidential libraries. She passed away in 1918 at the age of 85.

The Garfield family. James's mother is to the left, while Lucretia sits to the right. Four of their children are pictured behind them.

The couple are buried at the James A. Garfield Memorial in Cleveland, Ohio.

I somehow feel that the house is a much more interesting monument to your father's memory than anything that can be built merely as a monument, and I want it to be worthy of him.

The James Garfield National Historic Site

Ellen Harris Herndon Arthur

An only child, Ellen "Nell" Herndon was born in 1837 to William Lewis Herndon and Frances Elizabeth Hansborough. Born in Virginia, she spent large parts of her childhood in Washington, D.C. Her father was a naval officer, often away from home, and Ellen and her mother were very close as a consequence.

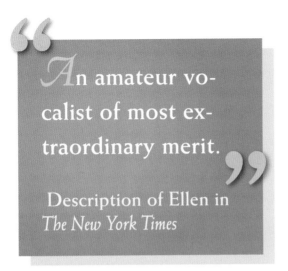

Ellen's father died in 1857. A year later, Ellen and her mother were visiting Saratoga Springs, New York, when a cousin introduced Ellen to Chester Arthur. The couple married in 1859 and lived in New York. They had three children: William Lewis, who died at the age of two; Chester Alan, Junior, and Ellen, dubbed "Nellie."

Ellen's father, William Lewis Herndon, was an explorer with the U.S. Navy. His ship went down in a hurricane in 1857.

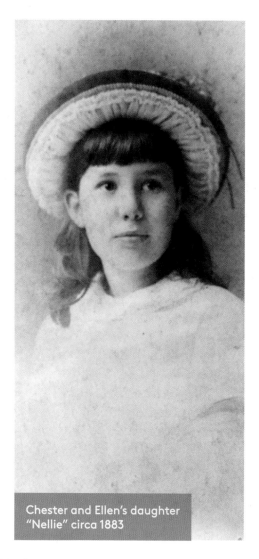

Chester and Ellen's daughter "Nellie" circa 1883

The Arthurs were a prominent New York couple, with Ellen's connections helping further Chester's political rise. They had shared political ambitions, although Chester's time away from home sometimes caused strife in their marriage.

In January 1880, Ellen contracted pneumonia and died at the age of 42. Later that year, Chester was chosen to run for vice president, and he became president in September 1881 when James Garfield died. Chester mourned his wife deeply, using rooms at the White House that allowed him to see the stained-glass window he'd installed at a nearby church in her memory. Early in Chester's presidency there was little entertaining, to honor Garfield. Chester's sister, Mary "Molly" McElroy, took over hosting duties from January 1883 onward.

> *"Honors to me now are not what they once were."*
>
> **Chester Arthur, following Ellen's death**

Chester Arthur's grave in New York

Circa 1897

Frances Folsom Cleveland Preston

Frances, nicknamed "Frank," was born in 1864 to Oscar Folsom and Emma Harmon. She had one younger sister who died in infancy. Grover Cleveland, a family friend more than twenty-five years older, knew her when she was a child. When Oscar Folsom died, Cleveland was an executor of Oscar's estate.

As a young woman, Folsom liked theater and photography. In spring of 1885, the year she graduated college, Grover Cleveland proposed. Newly engaged, Folsom spent much of the year after graduation traveling in Europe with her mother, a trip Grover Cleveland encouraged. He knew the press would scrutinize her closely and believed the trip would give her some polish before the marriage.

> "Mr. Cleveland, then governor of New York, began to send her flowers—which gifts became the subject of excited comment among her fellow students."
>
> *The Sedalia Democrat* newspaper, 1947

Frances Folsom and Grover Cleveland married during his first term in the White House.

The first White House presidential wedding took place in the Blue Room of the White House on June 2, 1886. Young and attractive, Frances became a fashion icon. Grover had hoped to protect his new wife from attention, but to little avail.

Rose Cleveland, Grover Cleveland's sister, served as his White House hostess before his marriage. Though Grover was of a different political party than his predecessor Chester Arthur, Rose was on good terms with Mary McElroy, Arthur's sister who served as his hostess.

While at the White House, Frances Cleveland started a tradition of hosting working women during Saturday receptions. The position of first lady was carrying with it a higher profile and voluminous correspondence, and Cleveland hired a social secretary out of the family's funds.

While Grover won the popular vote in the 1888 election, his opponent Benjamin Harrison won the election. But in a unique turn in American history, the Clevelands returned to the White House in 1893.

A contemporary newspaper illustration shows the bride with her mother at the White House wedding.

> ## "We are coming back just four years from today."
>
> **Frances Cleveland reportedly said this to White House staff as the couple left after his first term.**

Frances Folsom Cleveland is shown here with the wives of Grover Cleveland's Cabinet members.

An 1893 lithograph shows Frances and Grover with their oldest daughter, Ruth.

Frances and Grover had five children, three daughters and two sons. Ruth, born 1891, died tragically in 1904 of diphtheria. Esther was the first baby born at the White House in 1893.

In 1908, Grover Cleveland died, leaving 44-year-old Frances to raise their children.

She married an art history professor, Thomas Preston Jr., in 1913. Though opposed to female suffrage, Frances had an active public life. She supported entering World War I (1914–1918) and gave speeches to that effect, joined welfare charities, and was part of a needlework guild that was active during World War I and the Great Depression (1929–1939). The youngest first lady died in 1947, 51 years after leaving the White House.

<blockquote>
"**S**he is naturally a womanly woman and a gracious hostess, but her chief charm lies in the fact that she is an admirable listener."

Congressman quoted in Frances Preston's obituary
</blockquote>

A photograph taken between 1915 and 1920 is labeled "Mrs. T.J. Preston." Frances remarried in 1913.

Caroline Harrison, ca. 1885

Caroline Lavinia Scott Harrison

Caroline Lavinia Scott was born on October 1, 1832, the second of five children in Oxford, Ohio. She was an excellent and dedicated student, particularly in history. She adored music and art, becoming an accomplished pianist and painter.

Witty, charming, and talented, teenage Scott caught the heart of Benjamin Harrison while he was a young law student, and the two married on October 20, 1853. The couple settled in Indianapolis, Indiana, where they had two children, Mary and Russell Benjamin. They moved to Washington, D.C., when Benjamin Harrison became a senator, and moved into the White House when he became president in 1888.

The Harrisons' home in Indianapolis, Indiana

> *W*e have within ourselves the only element of destruction; our foes are from within, not without.

Caroline Harrison was dismayed at the state of the White House. Congress rejected her proposed additions to the mansion, so she instead organized an extensive renovation of the existing rooms. She also organized and cataloged historic White House objects, designed a new pattern for the presidential china, and brought in ferrets to conquer the building's rat problem.

Harrison helped found the Daughters of the American Revolution during her time as first lady, and she became its first president-general. She also raised significant funds for the Johns Hopkins medical school, granted only on the condition that they admit women.

Toward the end of her husband's term as president, Harrison contracted tuberculosis. She died of the disease on October 25, 1892, and was buried in Indianapolis.

Benjamin Harrison, 1895

Mary Harrison McKee, Harrison's daughter, who served as hostess after her mother's death

Harrison resented the attention she and her family garnered from the press while in the White House, saying:

"*I* have about come to the conclusion that political life is not the happiest—you are [so] battered around in it that life seems hardly worth living."

Portrait of Caroline Harrison, painted 1894

Ida Saxton McKinley

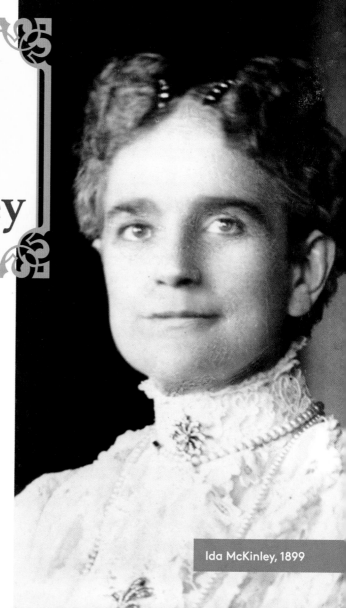

Ida Saxton was born into a wealthy, liberal family on June 8, 1847, in Canton, Ohio. Her grandfather, John Saxton, had founded Canton's first newspaper in 1815. Ida grew up with two siblings, Mary and George. Her father encouraged her to pursue college studies and work at his bank, an occupation

Ida McKinley, 1899

considered unsuitable for women at the time. Intelligent and willful, Ida and her sister went on a tour of Europe in 1869, during which Ida frequently butted heads with their chaperone. Ida met her future husband, William McKinley, at a picnic in Ohio in 1867. They began courting after Ida returned from Europe, and they married in 1871.

Ida and William McKinley, 1900

Ida S. M°Kinley.

66 *P*eople ought to travel to see how much there is to learn and read. 99

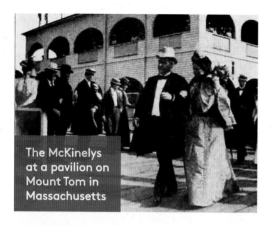

The McKinleys at a pavilion on Mount Tom in Massachusetts

In the early 1870s, Ida McKinley developed epilepsy and began suffering migraines. When she and her husband entered the White House in 1897, this limited her participation in some traditional first lady duties like hosting, but she was still involved in her husband's presidency. She listened to his political meetings from outside his office and then shared her thoughts with him. She travelled with William whenever she could, and she edited his speeches and helped steer him toward some White House appointments she supported.

McKinley believed in women's right to vote, and she often spoke about the topic at gatherings. When she was too ill to attend charity gatherings, she knit slippers to be auctioned off at the events.

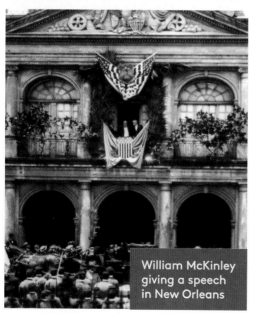

William McKinley giving a speech in New Orleans

McKinley, the year she became first lady

On handing lilies to suffrage supporters visiting the White House, McKinley said:

"*W*hen you go to the suffrage convention, I want you to tell them that this is from me, as a gift to all of you."

The McKinleys had two daughters, named Ida and Kate. Baby Ida died just months after she was born, and Kate died of typhoid fever when she was five years old. McKinley was devastated by these losses.

The McKinleys at their home in Ohio

The President McKinley Memorial, which Ida McKinley helped organize

" *H*e is gone, and life to me is dark now. "

In September of 1901, during the first year of William's second term in the White House, an assassin shot him. William died eight days later, on September 14. His body was interred in a vault at a cemetery in Canton, Ohio, which she visited daily. She also worked on a memorial for the deceased president. Six years later, on May 26, 1907, Ida died. She was interred in the vault next to her husband.

Edith Kermit Carow Roosevelt

Edith Carow was born August 6, 1861, in Norwich, Connecticut. As a child, friends and family called her "Edie." Her grandfather, Daniel Tyler, had been a Union general in the Civil War (1861–1865). She had a younger sister, Emily, and a brother, Kermit, who died a year before she was born.

Edith Roosevelt, ca. early 1900s

Roosevelt, 1903

While growing up in New York City, she lived next door to Theodore "Teddy" Roosevelt, who would later become her husband and president of the United States. They began a relationship as teenagers, but when Teddy attended Harvard University, he met and later married Alice Lee, with whom he had one daughter. Alice Lee died in 1884. A year later, Edith and Teddy began seeing one another and married in 1885.

Edith K. Roosevelt

" *I* think imagination is one of the greatest blessings of life. "

The Roosevelts at a reception after President McKinley's death

Edith Roosevelt served as second lady when Teddy Roosevelt was vice president under William McKinley. When President McKinley was assassinated early in his second term, Teddy assumed presidency and Edith became first lady. Edith Roosevelt helped provide important information for the negotiation of a treaty that stopped the Russo-Japanese War, earning her husband a Nobel Peace Prize in 1906. The Roosevelts became the first president and first lady to travel abroad when they visited the construction of the Panama Canal.

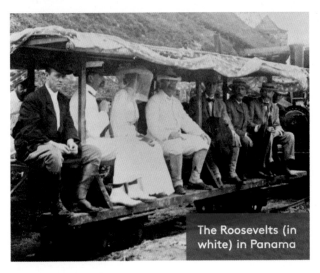
The Roosevelts (in white) in Panama

Teddy Roosevelt reportedly said of his wife to William Howard Taft:

"*I* take the keenest pride in seeing Mrs. Roosevelt at the head of the White House—a gentlewoman, who gives to all the official life . . . an air of gracious and dignified simplicity, and who with it all is the ideal of a good American wife and mother who takes care of her six children in the most devoted manner."

Edith Roosevelt created a new era in the White House. She hired a full-time social secretary and later created a staff that helped with dinners and other important activities. She also called regular meetings with Cabinet members' wives to talk about moral issues. Congress funded an expansion of the White House, which included creating the West Wing. The first lady had a large hand in the renovations.

Roosevelt, ca. 1890

Roosevelt, ca. 1904

White House west garden

"We're running out of funds."

— Edith Roosevelt, who was known for excellent money-management skills.

Roosevelt family, 1903

Edith and Teddy Roosevelt had five children: Theodore, Jr., Kermit, Archibald, Ethel, and Quentin. Edith Roosevelt also welcomed Teddy's child, Alice, from his first wife. The children spent many happy times frolicking on the lawn of the White House as well as playing antics inside, such as hiding behind potted palms, then jumping out to scare guests.

Roosevelt's Sagamore Hill home

Her husband's term in office ended on March 4, 1909, and the family returned to their home at Sagamore Hill in New York. Teddy died January 6, 1919, and Edith lived for another 29 years. She died on September 30, 1948 at the age of 87.

> "One cannot bring up boys to be eagles and expect them to be sparrows."

Theodore Roosevelt's gravesite, where Edith Roosevelt was later buried

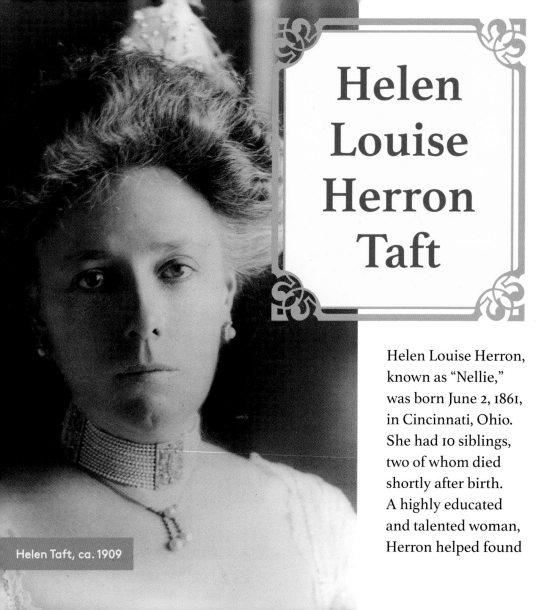

Helen Louise Herron Taft

Helen Taft, ca. 1909

Helen Louise Herron, known as "Nellie," was born June 2, 1861, in Cincinnati, Ohio. She had 10 siblings, two of whom died shortly after birth. A highly educated and talented woman, Herron helped found the Cincinnati Symphony Orchestra Association. Historians say she wanted to marry a man who appreciated her intelligence and who possessed the skills needed to become the nation's leader. In 1886, she married the future president of the United States, William Howard Taft.

The Tafts playing cards with friends during William's government posting in the Philippines

I believe in the best and most thorough education for everyone, men and women.

Taft (seated) and her daughter Helen, who took over hosting duties after the first lady's stroke

The Tafts in a carriage on their way to the White House on Inauguration Day

Historians have argued Taft's husband would never have become president were it not for Helen's own ambitions. In 1909, Taft was the first of any first lady to ride with the president to the White House on inauguration day. She suffered a stroke two months after the inauguration and could not be as involved politically as she wanted. Still, she worked to recover and was able to serve as one of her husband's most important advisers. The Tafts' grown daughter, Helen Manning, acted as hostess while her mother recuperated. In 1914, William Howard Taft lost his bid for re-election. But in 1921, he was appointed Chief Justice of the Supreme Court. Helen Taft became the only woman to be the wife of both a president and a chief justice.

The Tafts at the White House, ca. 1920

"" *I* think any woman can discuss with her husband topics of national interest.... I had always had the satisfaction of knowing almost as much as he about the politics and intricacies of any situation. ""

Cherry trees in Washington, D.C., today

As first lady, Taft supported federal legislation to ensure good conditions for workers. A bill reflecting her wishes passed in 1912. She also supported women's right to vote. Though the prohibition of alcohol was discussed during this time, she demonstrably opposed it and served White House guests alcohol. In 1912, Taft placed the first saplings of more than 3,000 Japanese cherry trees on the Capitol grounds. The wife of an ambassador from Japan, who gave the trees to the United States, helped with the first plantings.

Taft at the unveiling of a statue of Revolutionary War hero Friedrich Wilhelm von Steuben in 1910

" *I* became familiar with more than politics. It involved real statesmanship. "

Portrait of Helen Taft, taken during the Taft presidency

The Tafts raised three children: Robert, Helen, and Charles. The children lived in the Philippines with their parents when their father served as Governor-General there between 1901 and 1903. Robert later attended Harvard Law School. Helen received a scholarship to attend Bryn Mawr College, and later became the school's acting dean. Charles, the youngest, was the only child to live in the White House during the Taft presidency. He later earned a law degree at Yale.

The Taft family, ca. 1909

Arlington Cemetery

Taft remained active in Washington, D.C., even after her husband died in 1930. When she passed away 13 years later, in 1943, she was buried next to her husband in Arlington National Cemetery.

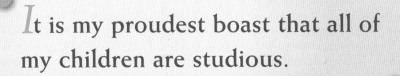

*I*t is my proudest boast that all of my children are studious.

Ellen Axson Wilson, ca. 1912

Ellen Louise Axson Wilson

Ellen Louise Axson was born on May 15, 1860, in Savannah, Georgia. She had two brothers and one sister. Her father, Edward Axson, was a Confederate chaplain during the Civil War (1861–1865). Well-educated and a lover of art, music, and literature, Ellen won numerous awards for her landscapes and drawings. Ellen met Woodrow Wilson in 1883. Though engaged five months later, they waited so Woodrow could finish graduate school at Johns Hopkins University and Ellen could care for her ailing father. They married on June 23, 1885. Just before she became first lady, Ellen Wilson had a one-woman art show of landscapes in Philadelphia.

Ellen A. Wilson

Prospect House, the Wilsons' home at Princeton University, painted by Ellen Wilson

> *"How can we best promote a fuller and more general appreciation of American art?"*

Ellen Wilson chose this question to be debated at an artist's colony she visited.

Ellen Wilson's husband relied on her skills in writing political speeches during his presidential campaign, and he had already seen her ability to arrange and manage social events when he served as president of Princeton University. Neither husband nor wife embraced entertaining while in the White House, but they understood its necessity. Wilson was well-read and understood political theory, which she used when discussing issues with her husband during his presidency. She's said to have helped clinch a compromise on a tax bill by inviting lawmakers to dinner at the White House. She also is noted for creating the White House rose garden, which today serves as a focal point for special gatherings.

Ellen Wilson, ca. 1912

White House garden
put in by Wilson

"You must not do it,"

Wilson told her husband when he considered withdrawing from the presidential primary election.

ELLEN LOUISE AXSON WILSON | 165

Ellen and Woodrow Wilson at a political event

As first lady, Wilson worked to improve life for Black Americans in Washington, D.C., and worked with social activist Charlotte Hopkins to promote legislation to this end. Wilson is said to have walked with key members of Congress through Black neighborhoods in Washington, D.C.

In 1914, the House and Senate passed a federal bill that set minimum housing standards in Washington, D.C. That same year, on August 6, Ellen Wilson died from kidney disease.

> "*N*obody who has not tried can have the least idea of the exactions of life here (at the White House) and of the constant nervous strain of it all."

©AMERICAN PRESS ASS'N N.Y.

The Wilsons, ca. 1910

The Wilson family

Wilson endured several years early in their marriage in which her husband was unfaithful, but the couple worked through it and raised three daughters. All three were grown by the time the Wilsons entered the White House. Upon her mother's death, the eldest daughter, Margaret, took on the role of first lady until her father remarried. Margaret never married and eventually moved to India, where she became Hindu. The Wilsons' middle daughter, Jessie, was active with League of Women Voters, and Eleanor married a United States secretary of the treasury. Wilson helped plan her two younger daughters' weddings at the White House while she was still alive.

When she was near death, Ellen Wilson said,

" Take good care of my husband. "

Wilson with her daughter Jessie

SACRED TO THE MEMORY OF
ELLEN LOUISE AXSON
BELOVED WIFE OF WOODROW WILSON
BORN 15 MAY 1860 AT SAVANNAH GEORGIA
DIED 6 AUGUST 1914 AT WASHINGTON D C

A TRAVELLER BETWEEN LIFE AND DEATH
THE REASON FIRM THE TEMPERATE WILL
ENDURANCE FORESIGHT STRENGTH AND SKILL
A PERFECT WOMAN NOBLY PLANNED
TO WARN TO COMFORT AND COMMAND
AND YET A SPIRIT STILL AND BRIGHT
WITH SOMETHING OF ANGELIC LIGHT

Ellen Wilson's gravestone

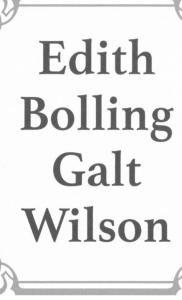

...lt, ca. 1913

Edith Bolling Galt Wilson

Edith Bolling was born on October 15, 1872, in Wytheville, Virginia. Edith was the seventh of eleven children in a family of slave-owners. Two of her siblings died during their infancy. Edith was not fond of her schoolwork, but she did enjoy her time at a school for girls in Richmond,

Virginia. She married her first husband, Norman Galt, who worked as a jeweler, in 1896. Norman died in 1908 when he was 43 years old, leaving Edith a widow. She met Woodrow Wilson during his first term as president, not long after his first wife, Ellen, had died in 1914. Edith and Woodrow wed on December 18, 1915.

Edith Bolling, a few years before marrying Norman Galt

Edith Bolling Wilson

Edith wrote a letter to Woodrow after his first proposal of marriage, which included:

" You can't love me, for you don't really know me; and it is less than a year since your wife died. "

The Wilsons in 1916

Edith Wilson served as the first lady during World War I (1914–1918). During the war, she worked with her husband to follow federal rationing recommendations by avoiding meat on Mondays and wheat on Wednesdays. They also brought in a herd of sheep to mow the White House Lawn so the White House groundskeepers could go to war. The Wilsons auctioned the sheep's wool to raise money for the American Red Cross and supported the purchase of war bonds.

During the war,

"*P*eople descended upon the White House until their coming and going was like the rise and fall of the tides. To achieve anything amidst such distractions called for the most rigid rationing of time."

Edith and Woodrow
Wilson, 1920

In 1919, Woodrow Wilson suffered a stroke that left him paralyzed on one side and blind in one eye. Edith Wilson kept her husband's condition secret as best she could from Americans. Neither she nor her husband wanted the presidential duties to be relinquished to the vice president. Wilson wrote in her memoirs that her husband's physician encouraged her to assume a stewardship role of the presidency. Historians debate whether she was the one running the presidency instead of her ill husband. Some historians argue Edith Wilson played a role, albeit one she did not plan, in the failure of the 1919 Treaty of Versailles, which her husband had supported.

> " *I* studied every paper sent from the different Secretaries or Senators and tried to digest and present in tabloid form the things that, despite my vigilance, had to go to the President. I, myself, never made a single decision regarding the disposition of public affairs. "

Edith Wilson gave birth to one child, who died in infancy, during her first marriage. She had no children with Woodrow Wilson. After Woodrow died in 1924, she wrote *My Memoir*, which covered her life as the first lady. She also established the Woodrow Wilson Foundation. Edith Wilson died on December 28, 1961, and is buried next to her husband at the National Cathedral in Washington, D.C.

Edith and Woodrow Wilson, 1919

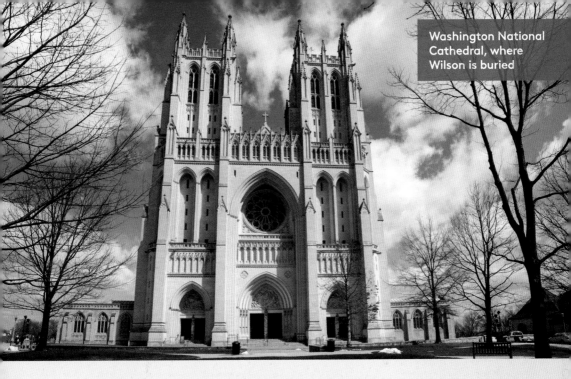

In *Madam President: The Secret Presidency of Edith Wilson*, author William Hazelgrove wrote:

"The president would have a severe stroke and leave her to run the United States government and negotiate the end of World War I. She was our first woman president."

Florence Mabel Kling DeWolfe Harding

Florence Harding in the 1910s

Florence Mabel Kling was born on August 15, 1860, the eldest of three children, in Marion, Ohio. Florence wanted to become a classic pianist, and she learned a great deal about business from her father, Amos. She eloped with

Henry DeWolfe in 1880, and they had a son, Marshall. The couple divorced, likely because DeWolfe was an alcoholic and abandoned his family. Florence's father took over the support of Marshall, and Florence went to work as a piano teacher. Despite her father's objections, Florence married Warren Harding in 1891, while he was publisher of *The Marion Star*, an Ohio newspaper. She helped him run the business. During their marriage, Warren had affairs with women, including one to whom hush money was supposedly paid.

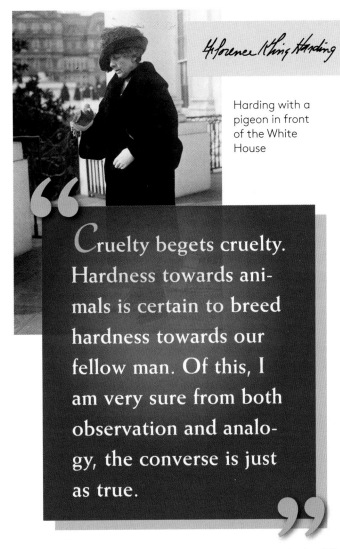

Harding with a pigeon in front of the White House

> *C*ruelty begets cruelty. Hardness towards animals is certain to breed hardness towards our fellow man. Of this, I am very sure from both observation and analogy, the converse is just as true.

Florence Harding as first lady,
likely with members of the military

Harding used her business knowledge to help her husband manage his calendar, finances, and speeches while he served as an Ohio state senator and, later, the lieutenant governor. She continued influencing her husband when he became president in 1921, making suggestions on Cabinet appointments and encouraging Andrew Mellon, a highly successful businessman, to agree to become secretary of the treasury.

"*W*ell, Warren Harding, I have got you the presidency. What are you going to do with it?"

Harding adjusts her husband's suit

Harding operating a newsreel camera with women journalists on the White House lawn

Wilson visiting the Tomb of the Unknown Soldier

As first lady, Harding focused on several issues. For example, she led a national boycott on sugar when it was too expensive for middle class people to afford it. She also supported the funding of the federal Alderson Reformatory Prison, which housed women. The women were taught skills to help them live on their own after leaving prison. She urged women across the country to become involved in politics, and supported women such as scientist Marie Curie, who visited her in the White House.

> " *L*et women know and appreciate the meaning of being an American— free and equal. "

Florence Harding in 1921

President Harding died while in office, likely of a heart attack. Admired by the public during his presidency, Warren's corruption and infidelity came to light after his death. Vice President Calvin Coolidge became president, and Florence returned to Ohio.

The Hardings had no children together. Florence's son with her first husband, Marshall, was raised by her parents. He died in 1915. She would not allow anyone to discuss her ex-husband or son while she was at the White House.

During her life, Florence suffered on and off from kidney disease. She died on November 21, 1924, in Marion, Ohio. Marshall's two children, George and Eugenia, inherited her estate.

Florence and Warren Harding
before the presidency

" *I* have only one real hobby—my husband. "

Grace Anna Goodhue Coolidge

Grace Anna Goodhue was born January 3, 1879, the only child of Andrew and Lemira Goodhue, in Burlington, Vermont. Unlike many women in her generation, Grace went to college, where she earned an undergraduate degree in teaching. After graduating, she worked at the Clarke School for the Deaf. She remained dedicated to the school after she left teaching, serving on its board for many years. Grace met Calvin Coolidge in 1904 and married him in 1905.

Coolidge called knitting a

" *S*tabilizer in time of perplexity or distress. "

Grace and Calvin Coolidge, ca. late 1910s

Grace Coolidge (center) and her husband (right) and son on Calvin's campaign trail

Even before their marriage, Calvin Coolidge showed his political ambitions, and Grace knew politics would be part of her life. She was with him as he began in lower political positions in Massachusetts, leading up to terms as governor and then U.S. vice president. Though Calvin preferred she didn't get involved in politics, he said that he needed Grace to be by his side to help him get through political and social matters.

Coolidge served as the second lady while her husband was vice president under Warren Harding, and then became the first lady after the unexpected death of Harding in 1923.

Coolidge sampling Girl Scout cookies, 1923

> *I*t has been my unbroken policy not to see newspaper writers or give interviews to anyone.

Grace Coolidge poses with a group of children at a White House event

The Coolidges outside the White House

Calvin Coolidge won a full term as president and was inaugurated in 1925, and the presidential couple chose not to have an inaugural ball.

Coolidge was known for her style, humor, and outgoing nature, and is still considered one of the nation's most popular first ladies. During her tenure in the White House, she supported the Red Cross by volunteering to visit disabled soldiers in hospitals. She also raised awareness of disabled Americans when she invited Helen Keller, a famous author who was both deaf and blind, to the White House. Coolidge remained dedicated to the Clarke School for the Deaf, but she strived to make sure she wasn't seen as showing any favoritism toward the school.

> " *T*here was a sense of detachment—this was I and yet not I. This was the wife of the President of the United States and she took precedence over me. "

Coolidge in her official White House portrait

Coolidge (left) talks with author and activist Helen Keller

Grace Coolidge holding her pet raccoon, Rebecca

The Coolidge family

The Coolidges had two sons, Calvin Jr. and John. One of their greatest tragedies was the loss of Calvin Jr. when he was only sixteen years old. The boy developed blood poisoning after playing tennis.

Grace Coolidge had a dog, Rob Boy, who is included in her White House portrait. In 1926, the Coolidges received a raccoon as a gift and raised it as a pet.

The Coolidges' son John lived until the year 2000, and helped create the President Calvin Coolidge State Historic Site.

In his autobiography,
Calvin Coolidge said of his wife,

"*F*or almost a quarter of
a century she has borne with
my infirmities, and I have
rejoiced in her graces."

Lou Henry Hoover

Lou Henry was born on March 29, 1874, in Waterloo, Iowa, the elder of two sisters. She loved nature and adventure, later earning a bachelor's degree in geology from Stanford University. It was at Stanford that she met Herbert Hoover, who also loved geology. He was working as a mining engineer in

Lou Hoover, ca. 1930

Australia when he wired a marriage proposal to Lou in California. They married on February 10, 1899, then traveled the world, following Henry's engineering jobs. In the process, they witnessed more than one world crisis. In 1900, they were in China for the Boxer Rebellion, and in 1914 they were in Europe for the outbreak of World War I. In both instances, the Hoovers organized food, shelter, and other aid for anyone who needed it.

Lou Henry on a burro in California, 1891

Lou Henry Hoover

> *I* was a Scout years ago, before the [Girl Scout] movement started, when my father took me fishing, camping, and hunting. Then I was sorry that more girls could not have what I had.

The Hoovers at a public event, 1932

Hoover did not play much of a part in her husband's presidential campaigns, and when they entered the White House, she assumed a somewhat quiet role as first lady. She did give speeches over the radio, the first of any first lady to do so. But she was generally not interested in talking with the media.

Early in the presidency, Hoover bought 164 acres of woods in Virginia to serve as a retreat for her and her husband. She named it Rapidan Camp. The Hoovers founded a school for impoverished families nearby.

The Hoovers at Rapidan Camp

> "*I* majored in geology in college but have majored in Herbert Hoover ever since."

The Cowboy Band welcoming Hoover, 1929

Hoover with a child, 1932

The Hoovers made changes to the White House while they were there. They moved furniture used by Abraham Lincoln to a special room, later known as the Lincoln Bedroom. Lou paid to have historic artifacts in the building catalogued, too. She also paid for college education for women, and she received multiple honorary degrees as first lady and beyond.

The Hoovers were in the White House at the start of the Great Depression in 1929, during which they received criticism when spending funds on entertainment. There is evidence, however, that the Hoovers had used their personal money and not government funds for these Depression-era events.

Chicago soup kitchen during the Depression

> *T*he one who is not in trouble will have to help the one who is in trouble.

Hoover hands out food baskets, 1932

Hoover with her sons

Hoover in front of the
White House with her dogs

The Hoovers had two sons, Herbert Charles and Allan Henry, both of whom became engineers. The eldest, Herbert, accompanied his parents on world travels when he was young. The family had many pets, some of them given as gifts. A family favorite was Pat, a German shepherd who was given to the Hoovers in May 1930. Pat wandered the White House grounds serving as patrol dog, and he later moved in with the Hoovers to their Palo Alto home in California, after they left the White House.

Lou Hoover died suddenly on January 7, 1944, in New York City. It was a full 20 years before her husband died, but he never remarried.

Herbert Hoover said that Lou was

" *A* symbol of everything wholesome in American life. "

The Hoovers, 1929

Anna Eleanor Roosevelt

Anna Eleanor Roosevelt was born October 11, 1884, in New York City, to parents Anna Hall and Elliot Roosevelt. With the same first name as her mother, Anna Eleanor preferred to go by her middle name. By the time she was ten years old, Eleanor's mother, one of her two brothers, and her father had all died.

Eleanor Roosevelt, 1932

Roosevelt in her wedding dress

Eleanor met her father's fifth cousin, Franklin Delano Roosevelt, in 1902. When they married on March 17, 1905, her uncle, then-President Theodore Roosevelt, walked her down the aisle. Their marriage nearly ended in 1918, when Eleanor discovered Franklin's affair with her former secretary. Franklin vowed to end the affair, however, and they chose not to divorce.

> *I*t is better to light a candle than curse the darkness.

Eleanor Roosevelt

Eleanor (second from right) with her father and brothers, 1892

The Roosevelts with the king and queen of England, 1939

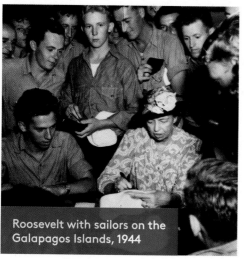

Roosevelt with sailors on the Galapagos Islands, 1944

When Franklin Roosevelt was elected to the presidency in 1933, the country was dealing with the Great Depression, and later, during his third term, the nation entered World War II (1939–1945). Throughout this time, Eleanor Roosevelt hosted a radio show, gave lectures, and wrote two columns. She toured Europe during the war to meet soldiers, visit hospitals, view downed planes, lay wreaths at soldiers' graves, shake thousands of hands, and support Black people serving in the war. She was greeted with cheers and claps, and said by one reporter to have a "modest and endearing personality."

On the day of the attack at Pearl Harbor, December 7, 1941, while her husband was meeting with the Cabinet, Eleanor Roosevelt spoke to the American public, saying:

> "Many of you all over this country have boys in the services who will now be called upon to go into action....You cannot escape anxiety. You cannot escape the clutch of fear at your heart and yet I hope the certainty of what we have to meet will make you rise above these fears."

Roosevelt with General Harmon and Admiral Halsey, 1943

Eleanor Roosevelt was the first first lady to appear before a congressional committee when she spoke about the deplorable conditions in public welfare institutions. She also vocally supported women's rights and opposed racial discrimination.

After her husband died during his fourth term, Eleanor Roosevelt went on to serve as chair of the United Nations Human Rights Commission and helped create the Universal Declaration of Human Rights.

Mary McLeod Bethune, Roosevelt, and others at the opening of a residence hall, 1943

"The battle for the individual rights of women is one of long standing and none of us should countenance anything which undermines it."

Roosevelt with members of the United Nations Women's Advisory Committee

The Roosevelts had six children. One, Franklin, died before his first birthday. The others were Anna, James, Franklin Delano, Elliott, and John, all married or in college when their parents moved to the White House. The large family visited often, and Roosevelt wrote about her children, grandchildren, and beloved pets in many of her columns about life at the White House. During the war, all four living sons fought as soldiers.

The Roosevelt family, 1919

Roosevelt with her dog Fala, 1952

In 1921, Franklin contracted an illness, possibly polio, that caused paralysis of his legs. Eleanor helped care for him until his death in 1945. She lived another nearly 20 years, dying in New York City on November 7, 1962.

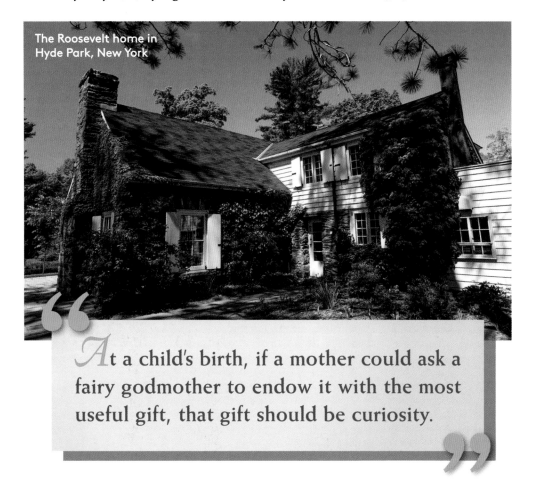

The Roosevelt home in Hyde Park, New York

"At a child's birth, if a mother could ask a fairy godmother to endow it with the most useful gift, that gift should be curiosity."

Elizabeth Virginia Wallace Truman

Bess Truman's official White House portrait

Elizabeth Virginia Wallace was born on February 13, 1885, in Independence, Missouri. Known as Bess or Bessie, she grew up with three brothers, and loved baseball and fishing. Bess also had a sister, though she died at about the age of three. After her father committed suicide in 1903,

Bess helped take care of the family with her mother.

Bess met Harry Truman when they were both children. They graduated from the same high school class, and married on June 28, 1919, just after he was discharged from the army, in which he served during World War I (1914–1918).

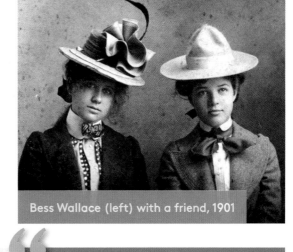
Bess Wallace (left) with a friend, 1901

Bess W. Truman

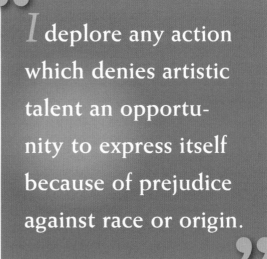
Bess Wallace at age four

> " *I* deplore any action which denies artistic talent an opportunity to express itself because of prejudice against race or origin. "

The Truman family on the campaign trail, 1948

Truman (left) and her daughter christening an airplane in 1945

Harry Truman, mostly unknown at the time, became vice president under President Franklin D. Roosevelt in January 1945. Just a short 82 days later, Roosevelt died, leaving Harry Truman to become president.

The nation was deeply involved in World War II (1939–1945) when Bess Truman became first lady. Unlike her predecessor, Eleanor Roosevelt, Truman preferred to keep her political thoughts private. Still, her husband considered her his "chief adviser," and often called her "the Boss." Despite this, she apparently was not aware when the president decided to drop the atomic bomb on Japan. Some historians argue she was upset that he did not consult her. Others have said she knew about the bomb, but the president didn't have time to tell her before thebomb hit.

> " *I* am not the one who is elected. I have nothing to say to the public. "

Truman with Michael Danna, a young representative of the Muscular Dystrophy Appeal Campaign, 1952

Truman receives an award for her service as the Girl Scouts of America honorary president, 1952

The Truman family

The Trumans had one daughter, Mary Margaret Truman, with whom they were very close. White House staff called the family the Three Musketeers. The trio listened to music, read, and discussed issues together. Margaret was ten years old when Harry Truman was elected Senator of Missouri, and she attended college when her parents were living in the White House.

Harry and Bess Truman were said to be very close and dedicated to one another. Harry died in 1972. Bess died ten years later, on October 18, 1982.

> *H*arry and I have been sweethearts and married more than forty years and no matter where I was, when I put out my hand Harry's was there to grasp it. "

The Trumans in front of the family home in Missouri

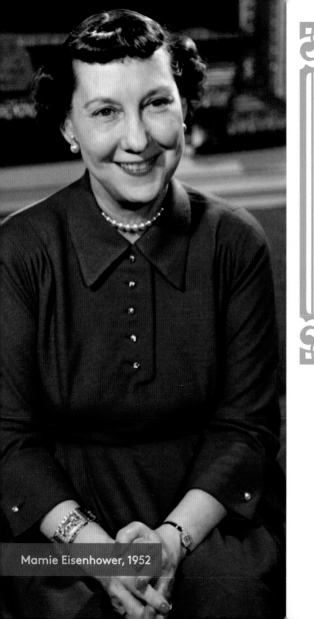

Mamie Eisenhower, 1952

Marie "Mamie" Geneva Doud Eisenhower

Marie "Mamie" Geneva Doud was born November 14, 1896, in Boone, Iowa. She grew up with three sisters in Denver, Colorado, and the family spent winters with relatives in Texas. Doud was not particularly interested in schooling, but her father taught her much about finances.

Mamie and Dwight Eisenhower, 1916

She became an army wife when she married Dwight D. Eisenhower on July 1, 1916. He gradually worked his way up from second lieutenant to five-star general, and then the president of the United States. Known as "Ike," Dwight is said to have loved his wife's saucy attitude.

Mamie Doud Eisenhower

Mamie's birthplace in Iowa

"*Television has tremendous power over our lives.*"

Mamie Eisenhower traveled with her husband during his presidential campaigns. The public was smitten with her and often shouted, "We want Mamie," after her husband had made his appearance. Ike was inaugurated for his first term in 1953, and Mamie enjoyed being the first lady and entertaining heads of state from other countries. As first lady, Eisenhower, who particularly loved the color pink, was named annually as one of the ten best dressed women in the United States and served as a role model for American women.

Mamie Eisenhower during her time as first lady

> **"** *I*'ve just had the first good night's sleep I've had since we've been in the White House. Our new bed finally got here, and now I can reach over and pat Ike on his old bald head any time I want to. **"**

The Eisenhowers celebrating Dwight's 1956 election victory

The Eisenhowers with Nikita and Nina Krushchev, 1959

Lucille Ball and Desi Arnaz

Mamie Eisenhower tended to make her views known in quiet ways. For example, she was in the White House when Senator Joe McCarthy claimed certain government officials and entertainers were traitors and communists. One couple charged with being communists was Lucille Ball and Desi Arnaz. Knowing this, Eisenhower invited Ball and Arnaz to a birthday party for her husband and asked them to sit with her and Ike during dinner as a quiet, but public, affirmation.

"*W*hy this comes naturally. I've been training for it for 36 years. When you're in the Army, you get used to chasing after your husband."

Camp David

Eisenhower helped create Camp David, named after her grandson, as a retreat for the president. She also took charge of administrative work in the White House after her husband suffered a heart attack in 1955, until he recovered.

Mamie and Dwight had two children: Doud, who died of scarlet fever just three years after he was born, and John, who served in the army and later as ambassador to Belgium. Mamie's mother sometimes lived in the White House with the Eisenhowers, and the grandchildren visited often, posing for photos for the press.

Baby Mamie Doud with her parents

Eisenhower with her grandchildren, 1952

The Eisenhower home in Gettysburg, Pennsylvania

" I t's in the home that everything starts. "

After spending two terms in the White House, the Eisenhowers retired to their farm in Gettysburg, Pennsylvania. They also traveled in Europe and spent some winters in Georgia.

Mamie Eisenhower died November 1, 1979, at the Walter Reed National Military Medical Center in Bethesda, Maryland.

Jackie, 1961

Jacqueline Lee Bouvier Kennedy Onassis

Jacqueline Lee Bouvier was born on July 28, 1929, in Southampton, New York. Known as Jackie, the future first lady studied ballet, learned several languages, and won national horse riding championships.

She graduated with a degree in French literature from George Washington University. Bouvier worked as photographer in 1951, and she met John F. Kennedy 1952. They married on September 12, 1953.

> "We should all do something to right the wrongs that we see and not just complain about them."

The Kennedys on their wedding day, 1953

Jackie, 1935

Jacqueline Kennedy

Upon moving into the White House in 1961, Jackie Kennedy's focus as first lady was to care for her husband and children. She made many foreign trips with her husband. Her ability to speak many languages and her affinity for different cultures gained her worldwide respect.

Kennedy quickly became known both in the United States and abroad for setting fashion trends. As first lady, she oversaw the restoration of the White House and created the position of curator. She also held many artistic performances there including opera, ballet, and Shakespearean plays, and wrote much of *The White House: An Historic Guide* after establishing a fine arts committee.

Kennedy at Taj Mahal in Agra, India, 1962

The Kennedys with diplomats in Mexico, 1962

Kennedy visiting Palm
Beach, Florida, 1961

The Kennedys with the
French culture minister
at the White House

66

*T*he one thing I do not want to be called
is First Lady. It sounds like a saddle horse.

99

The Kennedys arriving in Dallas the day of John's death, 1963

The extended Kennedy family leaving John Kennedy's funeral

On November 22, 1963, President John F. Kennedy was assassinated in Dallas, Texas. Jackie left the public eye to mourn, and soon after created the John F. Kennedy Presidential Library and Museum. Five years after John's death, Jackie married Aristotle Onassis, and she took the name Jacqueline Onassis. She lived much of the time in Greece with Aristotle, but she returned permanently to the United States when Aristotle died in 1975, accepting a job in New York as an editor.

> ## " *W*e are the only country in the world that trashes its old buildings. Too late we realize how very much we need them. "

The JFK Library and Museum in Boston, Massachusetts

The Kennedys and their two children, 1962

Jackie Kennedy had a miscarriage in 1955 and had a stillborn daughter in 1956. She gave birth to healthy baby Caroline in 1957, and a son, John Jr., two weeks after her husband was elected president. Another son, Patrick, was born in 1963, but he died two days later.

As a young mother, Kennedy spent time playing with and reading to her children. She raised them to be independent and modest, according to various accounts. When grown, her daughter, Caroline Kennedy Schlossberg, talked about a favorite memory of wearing a witch costume on Halloween in the Oval Office. The Kennedys also had a menagerie of pets while in the White House, including horses, dogs, a cat, a canary, hamsters, and two parakeets.

Jackie Kennedy Onassis lived to see her children grow up to adulthood. She died on May 19, 1994.

> **I**f you bungle raising your children, I don't think whatever else you do well matters very much.

Kennedy with her children, 1962

Burial place of John and Jacqueline Kennedy

Claudia Alta "Lady Bird" Taylor Johnson

Claudia Alta "Lady Bird" Taylor was born on December 22, 1912, in Karnack, Texas, and had two older brothers. She received her nickname when she was an infant; people declared to be as pretty as a "ladybird."

Lady Bird Johnson at the White House

Young Lady Bird Taylor, 1915

Lady Bird Johnson

Friends and family called her Lady, Bird, or Lady Bird the rest of her life. Taylor had two older brothers. Her mother died when she was only five years old.

An intelligent and driven woman, Taylor received two degrees, one in art history and another in journalism, graduating cum laude. Taylor met Lyndon Baines Johnson in September of 1934, when he was working as a congressional aide. They married barely two months after meeting, on November 17.

Lady Bird's childhood home in Texas

" *A*rt is the window to man's soul. "

Lyndon Johnson taking the oath of office after Kennedy's death, with his wife and Jackie Kennedy

Lyndon signing the Medicare Bill in 1965, his wife behind him

Lady Bird Johnson became first lady after the assassination of President John Kennedy in November 1963. Lyndon had been his vice president and took Kennedy's place. Lady Bird supported the president's "war on poverty", which he spoke of during a state of the Union speech in 1964. She also helped him establish Project Head Start in 1965 for preschool-aged children from low-income families. When she gave speeches, she was met with protests about the Vietnam War (1955–1975).

Johnson outside the family ranch, 1978

66 *A* little stress and adventure is good for you, if nothing else, just to prove you are alive. 99

Lady Bird Johnson's name will be indelibly linked with the beautification of the nation and the Lady Bird Johnson Wildflower Center in Texas. As first lady, she helped formulate the Highway Beautification Act, often called Lady Bird's Bill. Johnson and the interior secretary traveled more than 100,00 miles to national parks to promote the natural wonders of the United States. Their excursions included rafting, hiking, camping, walking through a rare forest, and visiting a Native American reservation.

In 1968, the Johnsons' time in the White House was given an end date when Lyndon unexpectedly decided not to seek re-election.

Johnson speaking at the Conference for the Beautification of Washington, D.C., 1965

Johnson planting a dogwood tree, 1965

"*W*here flowers bloom, so does hope."

Lady Bird Johnson Wild-flower Center outside Austin, Texas

The Johnsons with children and grandchildren at Christmas, 1968

Johnson suffered three miscarriages before having two daughters, Lynda Bird and Luci Baines, who lived in the White House when they were teenagers. Both got married in the White House. Various dogs, hamsters, and lovebirds lived with the family, including Yuki, who sang duets with President Johnson.

For her work on the beautification of the country, Lady Bird Johnson received the Presidential Medal of Freedom in 1977. Lady Bird Johnson died on July 11, 2007, in Austin, Texas.

> *Children are apt to live up to what you believe in them.*

Johnson, 1990

The Johnson family cemetery

Thelma Catherine "Pat" Ryan Nixon

Thelma Catherine Ryan was born March 16, 1912, in Ely, Nevada. Her family called her Pat because she was born just before St. Patrick's Day. Over the years, she's been called both Pat and Patricia.

Pat Nixon at the White House, 1970

Pat and Richard Nixon, 1960

She grew up with two brothers and attended the University of Southern California, paying for her schooling by working many different jobs. Ryan graduated cum laude and started teaching at a high school in Whittier, California, where she met and later married attorney Richard Nixon, in 1940.

Pat Nixon

> " You can do anything you put your mind to. "

The Nixons on the campaign trail

Pat Nixon shaking hands with a young fan in Georgia, 1972

Nixon, though not political in her early adult years and somewhat of an independent, began studying congressional records to understand her husband's opponents in his political races. She was the second lady for eight years when her husband served as vice president under President Dwight Eisenhower. Richard Nixon's first presidential campaign included his wife in slogans worn on buttons reading, "Pat for First Lady." Richard Nixon lost to John F. Kennedy, then ran and won in 1968, with Pat again very involved in his campaign.

Nixon is said to have told her husband to destroy secret tape recordings related to what would become the Watergate scandal. She also told Richard not to resign as he faced impeachment in 1974.

> You know I have great faith in my husband. I happen to love him.

Richard Nixon taking his oath of office, 1969

As first lady, Pat Nixon supported the Equal Rights Amendment, was pro-choice, and encouraged her husband to choose a female for the Supreme Court. She was also the first of any first lady to wear pants in public.

Less than a month after her husband took office, Nixon created a national volunteer program, and she invited the public to tour the White House and gardens. She also traveled extensively as first lady, including to Peru, where she took part in a movement to help citizens there who were recovering from a massive earthquake. She was awarded the Grand Cross of the Order of the Sun from the Peruvian government. Nixon visited South Vietnam, too, in 1969, flying in a helicopter over the war zone so she could visit soldiers. She was also the first of all first ladies to visit China.

Nixon visiting an earthquake-damaged village in Peru, 1970

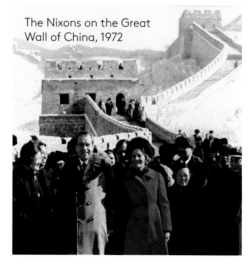

The Nixons on the Great Wall of China, 1972

"*I* know [student volunteers] are going to be great leaders of the future: They are going to solve all the problems of the world, not only of the country, but of the world."

Nixon with White House visitors, 1969

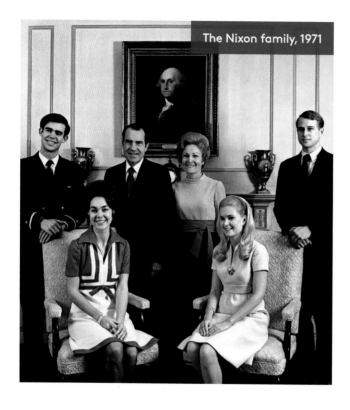

The Nixon family, 1971

The Nixons had two daughters: Patricia "Tricia" Nixon, and Julie Nixon, who married David Eisenhower, the grandson of President Dwight Eisenhower. It has been said that Pat Nixon kept her daughters' lives as private as possible, and Julie and David Eisenhower even decided against having a White House wedding.

The Nixons' daughters grew up before their father entered the White House. The family pet, a cocker spaniel that Tricia named Checkers, was received as a gift from a supporter in Texas. Checkers, the subject of one of Nixon's campaign speeches, sadly died before Richard Nixon was elected president.

Pat Nixon died June 22, 1993 in Park Ridge, New Jersey. Her husband Richard died less than a year later.

Pat and Richard dancing at their daughter's wedding, 1971

> *A*ll lives have triumphs and tragedies, laughter and tears, and mine has been no different.

Graves of Pat and Richard Nixon

Betty Ford, 1974

Elizabeth Anne Bloomer Warren Ford

Elizabeth Anne Bloomer, known as Betty, was born April 8, 1918, in Chicago, Illinois. The Bloomer family later moved to Colorado and then Michigan, where they spent summers at a family cabin.

Betty grew up with two brothers. She loved dancing and studied tap and ballet, hoping to become a professional. She married salesman William Warren in 1942, though they divorced five years later. She met lawyer Gerald Ford Jr. that same year, in 1947. They married on October 15, 1948.

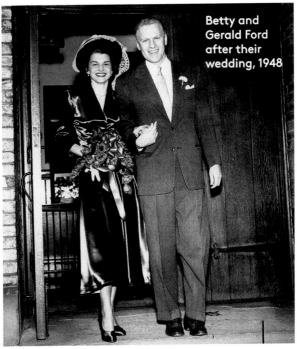

Betty and Gerald Ford after their wedding, 1948

Betty Bloomer, aged 18

Betty Ford

> *That's what we're here on Earth for, to help others.*

ELIZABETH ANNE BLOOMER WARREN FORD | 249

Gerald Ford was a congressman in 1973 when President Richard Nixon named him vice president, following the resignation of the previous vice president due to a financial scandal. After Nixon himself resigned in 1974, Gerald Ford took his place.

As first lady and beyond, Betty Ford supported the Equal Rights Amendment and abortion. With her husband, Ford visited Poland, Romania, and China. Ford discussed many issues with her husband and openly supported his pardon of Richard Nixon. Ford helped her husband campaign for a full term in 1977. He lost to Jimmy Carter.

Richard and Pat Nixon with Betty and Gerald Ford

Ford reads her husband's concession speech during the 1976 election

> **M**any barriers continue to the paths of most women, even on the most basic issue of equal pay for equal work."

A flag for the Equal Rights Amendment, playing on Betty Bloomer Ford's name

The Betty Ford Center

When she was diagnosed with breast cancer in September 1974, Ford was open about it with the public, and many women felt encouraged to have mammograms and send donations to the first lady, which she passed along to the American Cancer Society. She also raised funds for the Hospital for Sick Children in Washington, and for No Greater Love, which helped children whose parents were missing in action during the Vietnam War.

Ford is perhaps best known for founding the nonprofit Betty Ford Center in 1982, after she left the White House. The center helps people who struggle with substance abuse and addiction, and helps their families, as well. Ford herself long battled alcoholism and abuse of pain killers. She received the Presidential Medal of Freedom for her work in 1991.

"I thought I would hate being first lady. I love it."

Ford accepting the Presidential Medal of Freedom

ELIZABETH ANNE BLOOMER WARREN FORD | 253

The Fords had three sons: Michael, John, and Steven, and one daughter, Susan. The Fords opened the White House in 1975 to host the Holton-Arms School senior prom, which Susan attended. A golden retriever named Liberty and given by Susan to her father lived in the White House. Liberty gave birth to pups while living there.

Betty Ford died on July 8, 2011, in Rancho Mirage, California.

The Ford family in the Oval Office, 1974

The Fords riding a limo in Chicago, Illinois, 1974

> *H*olding these babies in my arms makes me realize the miracle my husband and I began.

A walkway outside the tomb of Betty and Gerald Ford

Eleanor Rosalynn Smith Carter

Rosalynn Carter, 1978

Rosalynn Carter was born Eleanor Rosalynn Smith in the small town of Plains, Georgia on August 18, 1927. She was the oldest of four children, and from the age of 13, she took a large role in caring for the family following the death of her father. She met Jimmy Carter, a friend's older brother, while they were both in school. They married in July 1946, shortly after she graduated junior college and a month before her 19th birthday.

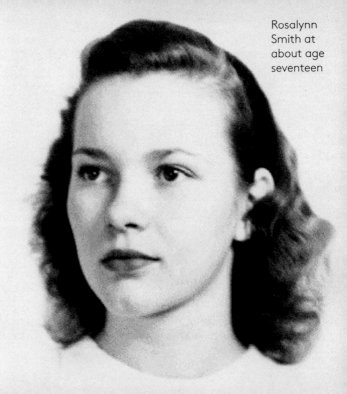

Rosalynn Smith at about age seventeen

Rosalynn Carter

" *T*here is clearly much left to be done, and whatever else we are going to do, we had better get on with it. "

ELEANOR ROSALYNN SMITH CARTER | 257

President Jimmy Carter and
First Lady Rosalynn Carter
at the 1977 Inaugural Ball

Carter took an active part in her husband's presidency, serving as a trusted
adviser and a political actor in her own right. One project she focused on
was the adoption of the Equal Rights Amendment (ERA), which guaranteed
equal rights regardless of gender. When Jimmy Carter took office in 1977,
the ERA was floundering. It had passed in Congress in 1972, but it needed
38 states to ratify it by 1981 and only 35 states had. Rosalynn Carter fought
to increase the amendment's popularity, but the ERA was still not ratified
by the time the Carters left the White House in 1981. The failure was one of
Rosalynn Carter's greatest disappointments.

> *I* had already learned from more than a decade of political life that I was going to be criticized no matter what I did, so I might as well be criticized for something I wanted to do.

Rosalynn Carter, Betty Ford, and other supporters of the Equal Rights Amendment at a rally

A ceremony welcoming Rosalynn Carter back from a 1977 international tour

One of Carter's biggest efforts has been her work regarding mental health. She found early in her political career that the effects of mental health were wide-reaching and largely ignored. In response, she has worked hard both during and after her husband's tenure as president to improve resources for those suffering mental illness, their loved ones, and their caregivers. As part of this work, she established the Rosalynn Carter Institute for Caregiving at Georgia Southwestern State University.

Carter testifies before a Senate subcommittee on behalf of the President's Committee on Mental Health

"Many politicians, celebrities, businessmen and women, and community leaders now are open about their struggles with mental illnesses, something almost unheard of when I began. Together, we are spreading the word that mental health affects all of us and deserves our support and attention."

Rosalynn Carter with her daughter Amy at the White House. Amy was the only child to live at the White House during the Carter presidency.

At home, Carter was devoted to her family. Her first four children, all sons, were born while her husband was serving in the Navy, and the family followed him from base to base. John William was born in Virginia in 1947, followed by James Earl III in Hawaii in 1950, and Donnel Jeffrey in Connecticut in 1952. The family returned to Plains, Georgia, to take over Jimmy Carter's family farming business in 1953, and their last child, Amy Lynn, was born there in 1967.

Carter family Christmas portrait, 1978

"*D*o what you can to show you care about other people, and you will make our world a better place."

Nancy
Davis
Reagan

Anne Frances Nancy
Robbins was born on July
6, 1921, in Manhattan,
New York. An only child,
she was often called
Nancy. Her parents di-
vorced soon after she was
born. Her mother later
married Dr. Loyal Davis,
who adopted Nancy and
changed her legal name
to Nancy Davis. Nancy

Nancy Reagan in
the White House
Red Room, 1981

Davis majored in English and drama at Smith College in Massachusetts, and pursued an acting career, eventually moving to California, where she met Ronald Reagan. They married on March 4, 1952.

Nancy Reagan

Nancy and Ronald Regan at their wedding

Nancy Davis, ca. 1950

" There's a big wonderful world out there for you. It belongs to you. "

The Reagans during the 1981 inaugural parade

As first lady, Reagan influenced her husband on many fronts. For example, she suggested he hold summit conferences with Mikhail Gorbachev, the Soviet general secretary at the time. The summits led to Reagan and Gorbachev signing a nuclear arms control treaty in 1987. When an assassination attempt was made on the president in 1981, Reagan began what the press would call her role as "chief protector" of her husband.

Mikhail and Raisa Gorbachev visiting the White House, 1987

> " *I*'m a woman who loves her husband and I make no apologies for looking out for his personal and political welfare. "

Nancy and Ronald Reagan speaking to the press, 1987

Reagan's most memorable project as first lady was the Just Say No drug awareness campaign she initiated in 1982. She traveled through the United States delivering her message that children should be taught to "Just Say No" when offered drugs. Reagan visited drug abuse prevention and rehabilitation centers, and even appeared in cameo roles on television shows to further her cause. When her husband was diagnosed with Alzheimer's disease after he finished his two terms in the White House, she actively supported the National Alzheimer's Association.

Reagan speaking at a Los Angeles "Just Say No" rally

> "Drugs take away the dream from every child's heart and replace it with a nightmare."

Reagan at a "Just Say No" event

Nancy and Ronald Reagan had two children: Patricia, who later took on the professional name Patti Davis, and Ron. Nancy Reagan was also a stepmother to Maureen and Michael Reagan, her husband's children with his first wife, Jane Wyman. Nancy Reagan and her daughter, Patti, had a difficult relationship, and at times were estranged. After Ronald Reagan developed Alzheimer's disease, mother and daughter reunited, and their relationship flourished.

Nancy Reagan died on March 6, 2016, in Los Angeles.

The Reagan family, ca. 1967

Nancy and Ronald Reagan, ca. 1990

After her mother's death, Patti Davis said,

"If a band of gypsies came and took me and Ron away, [her parents] would miss us, but they would be fine. It didn't mean they didn't love us... They were complete unto each other. That can be a complicated thing for children."

Barbara Bush, 1989

Barbara Pierce Bush

Barbara Pierce was born June 8, 1925, in New York City. She had a younger brother and older sister. Bush was an avid reader, swimmer, and tennis player. She met George H. W. Bush at a dance in Connecticut when she was 16 years old. They got engaged just before George went to serve in World War II (1939–1945).

The couple were married January 6, 1945, and remained wed for 73 years, until Barbara Bush's death on April 17, 2018.

Barbara Bush

"*N*ever lose sight of the fact that the most important yardstick of your success will be how you treat other people."

The Bush family, 1950

Bush lived with her husband in China when he headed the U.S. Liaison Office there. They returned to the U.S. three years later when George was named Director of Central Intelligence.

Bush served as second lady for eight years during President Ronald Reagan's two terms. When her husband began campaigning for the presidency, Bush steered clear of political issues. Though she rarely disagreed with her husband in public during his presidency, she made it known, mostly subtly, that she supported abortion, civil and LGBTQ rights, and gun control. Bush also supported the Gulf War started by her husband. The Bushes spent Thanksgiving in Saudi Arabia with troops. The couple left the White House when Bush lost his bid for re-election.

The Bushes in China, 1975

Barbara and George Bush with outgoing president Ronald Reagan

> *I* firmly believe we cannot tolerate discrimination against any individuals or groups.

George Bush takes the oath of office, 1989

Bush reading to children at a school in Missouri, 1991

Bush's major legacy was her unwavering support of family literacy, which she began promoting when she was second lady. She created the Barbara Bush Foundation for Family Literacy in 1989. A national radio program, "Mrs. Bush's Story Time," featured the first lady reading aloud to children. Bush also supported programs for the homeless, the elderly, and people with AIDS.

> **"** *I*f more people could read, write, and comprehend, we could be much closer to solving many of the other problems our country faces today. **"**

Bush visiting patients at the Children's Hospital in Washington, D.C., 1990

Barbara and George Bush with their children, early 1960s

Gravesite of Barbara Bush and her husband

Barbara and George Bush had six children, including George W., who served as the 43rd president of the United States, and Jeb Bush, who served as 43rd governor of Florida. A daughter, Robin, died of leukemia at age three. Their other three children were Neil, Marvin, and Dorothy. During the White House years, Barbara Bush was often seen with her pet English spring spaniel Millie, about whom she wrote a children's book.

Bush passed away in Houston, Texas, on April 17, 2018.

The extended Bush family, 2005

"Your success as a family, our success as a society, depends not on what happens in the White House, but on what happens inside your house."

Hillary Diane Rodham Clinton

Hillary Diane Rodham was born October 26, 1947 in Chicago, Illinois, and was raised with two younger brothers in nearby Park Ridge. During high school, Rodham swam and played softball, and she became a National Merit Finalist, graduating in the top five percent of her class.

Hillary
Rodham,
1965

Rodham earned a law degree from Yale University in 1973. She met future Bill Clinton while they were both in law school. They were married on October 11, 1975.

Hillary Rodham Clinton

"When you're knocked down, get right back up and never listen to anyone who says you can't or shouldn't go on."

Rodham in college, 1968

The Clintons on the campaign trail in 1992

Clinton reads to children at a bookshop, 1998

It made sense that Hillary Clinton, an active lawyer, speaker, and politician, would become heavily involved with her husband's presidency. Clinton established her own office in the West Wing, a first for first ladies. Clinton helped Bill choose some top-level administrators and chaired a task force on national health care reform, though her plan was never put to a vote. Clinton was still instrumental in getting the Adoption and Safe Families Act and Foster Care Independence Act passed. She also brought the issue of the treatment of Afghan women to the forefront and helped form Vital Voices, which promoted female participation in politics worldwide.

> *Every woman deserves the chance to realize her God-given potential.*

Hillary and Bill Clinton at a 1997 inaugural ball

Clinton testifying at the congressional hearing on health care reform, 1993

In 1996, Clinton wrote the *New York Times* best-selling book, *It Takes a Village: And Other Lessons Children Teach Us*. During a book tour, reporters often asked her about controversies that surrounded the White House, including allegations of conflict of interest, which never led to any charges. Clinton also endured a major scandal regarding her husband's affair with a White House intern. Clinton was both praised and criticized for her decision to remain married.

After the Clintons left the White House, Hillary Clinton served in the U.S. Senate for eight years, then became the Secretary of State under President Barack Obama after losing her own bid for the presidency. She ran again in 2016 and lost against Donald Trump.

Clinton with President Barack Obama during her time as secretary of state, 2009

Clinton on the campaign trail before the 2016 presidential election

Clinton is sworn in as a senator, 2001

" The most difficult decisions I have made in my life were to stay married to Bill and to run for the Senate from New York. "

The Clinton family, 2010

The Clintons have one daughter, Chelsea. Hillary restricted access to her daughter during the White House years. Clinton's mother, Dorothy Rodham, and her two brothers often spent weekends and holidays at the White House. The Clinton pets, Socks, a cat and Buddy, a dog, were often photographed by the press.

The Clinton family celebrate Bill's election victory, 1992

> *L*et's learn from the wisdom of every mother and father who teaches their daughters there is no limit on how big she can dream and how much she can achieve.

The Clinton family on Hillary's campaign trail 2016

Laura Bush, 2005

Laura Lane Welch Bush

Laura Lane Welch was born November 4, 1946, in Midland, Texas. A lifelong lover of reading and education, she obtained a bachelor's degree in education and a master's degree in library science. She went on to work as both a teacher and librarian. She met the future George W. Bush in 1977 at a barbecue, and they married later that year.

The Bush family, 1990

Laura Bush served as first lady of Texas starting in 1994, while her husband was governor, and she delivered the keynote address at the 2000 Republican National Convention when her husband was named a Republican presidential candidate. Bush supported her husband through two presidential terms, including during the September 11, 2001, terrorist attacks on the World Trade Center. Following the tragedy, Bush wrote many letters to American families to offer words of wisdom on helping young children who were afraid and worried.

The Bushes with John and Cindy McCain at a campaign rally, 2000

The Bushes talk with advisers following the September 11 attacks, 2001

" We need to reassure our children that they are safe in their homes and schools. We need to reassure them that people love them and care for them, and that while there are some bad people in the world, there are many more good people. "

The Twin Towers in New York City burn after the September 11 attacks, 2001

Bush at the opening of the 2001 Book Festival

Bush meets women in Abu Dhabi, United Arab Emirates, in 2007

As first lady, Bush spent much of her time on education, speaking to a Senate committee about increasing teacher salaries. She also began "Ready to Read, Ready to Learn," which focused on literacy for young children. In 2006, she hosted the Conference on Global Literacy. Bush also worked on women's health and wellness issues, and reached out to women nationwide to teach them about heart disease and its symptoms. Bush also made a radio address about the oppression of women in Afghanistan.

> " *E*very child in American should have access to a well-stocked school library. "

Bush after a reading for children, 2006

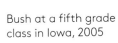

Bush at a fifth grade class in Iowa, 2005

George Bush takes the oath of office, 2005

Laura Bush gave birth to two fraternal twin daughters, Barbara and Jenna, in 1981. The twins were cited for underage drinking in 2001, during the first year of their father's first term as president. It was difficult news, as Laura Bush had helped George Bush quit drinking when he was 40 years old. Today, Barbara Bush, namesake of her grandmother who was a former first lady, is co-founder and chairwoman of the board of the Global Health Corps. Jenna, a journalist, is co-host of a morning news program.

During their White House years, Laura and George Bush doted on three dogs, Spot, Barney and Miss Beasley, a gift to Laura from George.

> " As parents, the most important thing we can do is read to our children early and often. Reading is the path to success in school and life. When children learn to love books, they learn to love learning. "

Laura and George Bush on their ranch in Texas, 2014

Michelle LaVaughn Robinson Obama

Michelle LaVaughn Robinson was born on January 17, 1964, in Chicago, Illinois. Her father, who had multiple sclerosis, worked for the Chicago water department while her mother stayed home to care for her and her older brother. Robinson

Michelle Obama during her time as first lady

earned a Bachelor of Arts from Princeton University and a law degree from Harvard University. She met Barack Obama when she was working at a Chicago law firm. They went on their first date in 1989, and they married on October 3, 1992.

Michelle Obama

The Obamas dance at an inaugural ball, 2009

66 *Y*our story is what you have, what you will always have. It is something to own. 99

MICHELLE LAVAUGHN ROBINSON OBAMA | 297

Michelle Obama speaks at a rally for Barack, 2008

Barack Obama taking the oath of office, 2009

Obama already accomplished a great deal well before her husband became president. She was the founding executive director of the Chicago Chapter of Public Allies, which helps young people prepare for public service, and she served as vice president of community and external affairs for the University of Chicago Medical Center. She relinquished some of her public service work to campaign with her husband in 2008. When he won, she became the first Black first lady in American history. She supported her husband's policies by hosting meetings and speaking about issues. One legislation she supported was the Lilly Ledbetter Fair Pay Act of 2009. Obama also stood with her husband to publicly favor same-sex marriage.

The Obama's celebrate Barack's election as president, 2008

> "Serving as your First Lady is an honor and a privilege."

The White House lit in rainbow colors to celebrate the legalization of gay marriage, 2015

As first lady, Obama created new programs, such as Let's Move to help children exercise more and eat healthier foods. Barack Obama created a childhood obesity task force to help promote that program. Michelle Obama also started a garden for children on the White House grounds, whose produce was used to make meals and to donate to food pantries. The first lady also created the Reach Higher Initiative to help youngsters continue their education after high school. In addition, working with Second Lady Dr. Jill Biden, Obama established Joining Forces to help veterans and their families.

Obama with children at a Let's Move event, 2013

Obama helping children garden outside the White House, 2013

> " *E*very day, the people I meet inspire me. Every day they make me proud. Every day they remind me how blessed we are to live in the greatest nation on earth. "

The Obamas with Vice President Joe and Dr. Jill Biden at the Lincoln Memorial, 2009

The Obama family, 2011

The Obamas have two daughters. Malia was born in 1998, and Sasha, the second youngest child ever to live in the White House, was born in 2001. Though they knew moving to the White House would be a big change for their daughters, the Obamas worked to keep their girls on a regular schedule with specific times to go to bed and do their homework.

The sisters got their wish for a puppy when they moved to the White House. The family adopted a Portuguese Water Dog named Bo, and a few years later, another one named Sunny. The Obama daughters were named two of the 25 most influential teens of 2014 by *Time Magazine*.

> *I* wake up every morning in a house that was built by slaves, and I watch my daughters, two beautiful, intelligent, Black young women, playing with their dogs on the White House lawn. "

The Obama family and their dog, Bo

Obama with her daughters outside the White House

Melania Knauss Trump

Melania Knauss was born April 26, 1970, in Slovenia, which was part of Yugoslavia at the time. Her older sister, Ines, is an artist. She also has an older half-brother, whom she is said to have never met. Knauss studied architecture and design in college, then began working as a fashion model in Europe before moving to New York City to continue her career. She met Donald Trump, who was 24 years older than she, at a party in 1998. They married in 2005. It was her first marriage and Donald Trump's third. A year later, Melania Trump became an American citizen.

> "As citizens of this great nation, it is kindness, love, and compassion for each other that will bring us together."

The Trumps at the Fashion Group International's Night of Stars, 2005

The Trumps at a 2017 inaugural ball

Melania Trump was not very involved in her husband's campaign for the presidency in 2016. She did, however, make her voice heard about bullying, and spoke to a crowd about the issue five days before the election. As first lady, she met with social media firms to talk about Internet safety. She also accompanied her husband to Texas to visit survivors of a mass shooting in a hospital. On January 18, 2021, she gave a farewell speech to Americans before she and her husband left the White House. Trump thanked members of law enforcement, healthcare professionals, teachers, and other essential workers amid the COVID-19 pandemic.

Trump meets victims of a shooting in El Paso, Texas, 2019

> " *V*iolence is never the answer. "

Trump takes part in a discussion about COVID-19 with hospital officials, 2020

Trump's campaign as first lady was known as the "Be Best" initiative, meant to promote emotional and physical health for children. She visited the Children's Inn, which helps children battling severe illnesses, each Valentine's Day, and helped collect donations to create a healing space at the Children's National Health System.

Trump visited Ghana, Malawi, Kenya, and Egypt in October of 2018 without her husband. She visited children there. She also placed a wreath at what once served as a slave outpost, where people were herded onto boats to be sold across the Atlantic Ocean.

Trump left the White House with her husband after he lost his bid for a second term to Joe Biden. Going against tradition, she did not ask the future first lady for a visit to the White House.

Trump with children at a Be Best event, 2019

Trump visits children at the National Institute of Health, 2019

> " I have been moved by children I have visited in hospitals and foster care centers. Even as they . . . face challenges, they bring such a joy to everyone they meet. "

Trump with children in Limuru, Kenya, 2018

Melania, Donald, and Barron Trump return from a trip to New Jersey, 2019

Melania and Donald Trump have one son, Barron, born in 2006. When Barron's father became president, he and his mother remained in New York City until he finished his schooling. Mother and son moved to the White House in June 2017.

Melania Trump has been said to get along well with Trump's other children from previous marriages, and considers them her friends.

> *I* think it is important to give a child room to make mistakes in order to learn. Mistakes build wings so later in life they can fly and go on their own.

The Trump family at Donald's inauguration

Jill Biden, 2009

Dr. Jill Tracy Jacobs Stevenson Biden

Dr. Jill Tracy Jacobs was born on June 3, 1951, in Hammonton, New Jersey. Four younger sisters followed. Jill earned a bachelor's degree in English and her doctorate in education. She now teaches writing at Northern Virginia Community College.

Jill married Bill Stevenson in 1970, and they divorced in 1975. She later met the future president Joe Biden, who had lost his wife and 13-month-old daughter in a car accident in 1972. Jill and Joe married on June 17, 1977.

> *E*ducation teaches us compassion and kindness, connection to others.

Jill Stevenson and Joe Biden, not long after they met in the 1970s

Jill Biden

Dr. Biden served as the second lady for eight years while her husband was vice president under Barack Obama. During these years, Dr. Biden visited more than 35 countries to promote community colleges and economic equality for women. She also visited hospitals and refugee camps, and began a cancer education project. She became good friends with Michelle Obama, and they created "Joining Forces" to help military families.

Michelle Obama and Dr. Biden in Haiti, 2010

Dr. Biden visiting a women's center in Marrakech, Morocco, 2014

> *I*n the past, there has been a stigma surrounding community colleges, where they were seen as a less viable option because they are not four-year universities. I know differently and so do the millions of people across the country who have received an affordable, quality higher education at community college.

Dr. Biden speaking at a campaign event before the 2019 presidential election

Dr. Biden took time off from teaching to campaign with her husband during the 2020 presidential election. She spoke about the effects of the COVID-19 pandemic on teachers, students, and parents. She also stressed that science should dictate how the pandemic would be controlled.

As first lady, Dr. Biden vowed to be active, helping her husband when needed. She also said she will continue working to fight cancer, promote education, and help military families. Dr. Biden is the first of any first lady to work full-time during her tenure. She told her husband she wanted to continue teaching during his presidency, and he supported her.

> *T*eaching isn't just what I do. It's who I am.

Dr. Biden at an English teacher's workshop in Ho Chi Minh, Vietnam, 2015

Dr. Biden talks with people at a health center during the COVID-19 pandemic, 2021

The Bidens have a daughter Ashley, born in 1981, who grew up to become a social worker, activist and fashion designer. Joe Biden also had two sons with his first wife, Beau and Hunter. In 2012, Dr. Jill Biden wrote *Don't Forget, God Bless Our Troops*, a book about her Beau's deployment to Iraq. In 2015, Beau died of brain cancer. After the tragedy, the Bidens established the Biden Foundation and Biden Cancer Initiative.

Though their children do not live with them in the White House, the Bidens did bring their two German Shepherds to live with them at the White House.

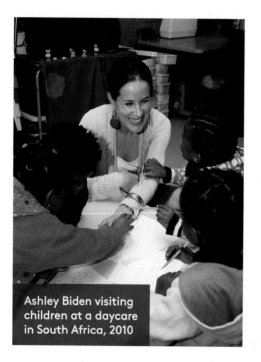

Ashley Biden visiting children at a daycare in South Africa, 2010

Beau Biden celebrates his election as Attorney General in Deleware, 2006

> *I* worry about my children worrying about me, feeling like they need to be the strong ones. It's not the right order of things.

Dr. Biden, her granddaughter, and the White House groundskeeper with dogs Major and Champ

The Bidens on Valentine's Day, 2021